LADY PRECIOUS STREAM

One of the most fruitful sources of inspiration for the modern theatre in the West has been the traditional Chinese drama. *Lady Precious Stream* is a Chinese play adapted for the English stage. It is a four-act play about Wang Yun the prime minister of a Chinese emperor's court and his wayward daughter, Lady Precious Stream, who marries a gardener. The play is based on traditional scenes which have been put together in such a way as to convey the whole atmosphere and effect of the Chinese drama.

The play was first staged in London in 1934 and this full acting edition with complete details of the staging, properties, lighting etc. has been in print for over thirty years. *Lady Precious Stream* has long since established itself as a classic in the repertoire of the English theatre.

The photograph on the front cover shows a scene from the original production at the Little Theatre and is reproduced by courtesy of the Raymond Mander and Joe Mitchenson Theatre Collection.

Lady Precious Stream

AN OLD CHINESE PLAY DONE INTO ENGLISH ACCORDING TO ITS TRADITIONAL STYLE

BY

S. I. HSIUNG

ACTING EDITION

EYRE METHUEN LTD
11 NEW FETTER LANE EC4

Originally published July 12th, 1934
Acting Edition first published June 1938
Reprinted nine times
This revised edition first published 1968
Reprinted 1971 and 1977

Copyright (*Acting Edition*) *1936 by S. I. Hsiung*

Printed Offset Litho and bound in Great Britain
by Cox & Wyman Ltd., London, Fakenham and Reading

ISBN 0 413 38740 2

The fee for each and every performance by amateurs in the British Isles is Code H, payable in advance to—

MESSRS. SAMUEL FRENCH, LTD.,
26 SOUTHAMPTON STREET,
STRAND, LONDON, W.C.2,

or their authorized agents, who, upon payment of the fee, will issue a licence for the performance to take place.

No performance may be given unless this licence has been obtained.

The costumes and wigs used in the performance of the play may be obtained from MESSRS. CHARLES H. FOX, LTD., 25 Shelton Street, London, W.C.2.

Other inquiries regarding this play should be addressed to ERIC GLASS LTD., 28 Berkeley Square, London W1X 6HD.

INTRODUCTION

It is a general belief in the West that the Chinese language is so complicated that the books published in Shanghai are not likely to be understood by the people in Peking. During a recent evening gathering of the London P.E.N. a gentleman asked me what language I used in my writings, the Northern or the Southern? I replied that there is no difference in writing but a little in speaking, just as the Welsh or Scottish accent differs from that of London. He was furious, and thought I was talking through my hat. I told him that I have been writing for the public for the past fifteen years and I ought to know my own language. Moreoever, I lived in Peking and nearly all my books were published in Shanghai! When I asked him had he ever been to China and did he know and speak the language at all, he said 'No!'

The belief here about the Chinese Drama is the same. For, no sooner was this argument settled than another dispute regarding the Drama arose. Someone, on hearing that I had written for the Chinese stage, remarked that a Chinese play generally lasts a fortnight. His neighbour corrected this statement by maintaining that it lasts three weeks! I tried to remove their misunderstanding by saying that both were far from the truth and that a Chinese play is no longer than a Western one, seldom longer than *Strange Interlude*, and never longer than *Back to Methuselah*! To my surprise, they gave up their difference and joined forces in attacking me. Almost everybody agreed with them, and it seemed that it was unanimously carried that a Chinese play must at least last a whole week, otherwise it would not be considered a real Chinese play!

A stage performance in China, indeed, is longer than one here. It begins at six or seven in the evening and ends about midnight. But it is what we call here a 'triple bill' of eight or nine acts from an equal number of different plays. As no drop-curtain is used, a Western visitor is liable to mistake the acting as of one continuous play.

Though the second act of the play *Lady Precious Stream* has moved thousands to tears and the third and fourth have delighted millions, these acts were, as a rule, performed separately and rarely produced as a whole play. In the unprintable slang of our green-room, we call this play 'The Eight Acts about the Wang Family'. We would select any of the two scenes of the second act for a programme which we did not wish to be too hilarious, or any of the third and the fourth for one which we did not wish to be too solemn. We follow our conventions so closely that we neglect the fact that many plays are in themselves sufficient to supply all that we require.

The conventional Chinese stage is not at all realistic. Apart from its lack of scenery, the indispensable property man is the greatest obstacle to realism. He is generally attired in his everyday habit and walks to and fro among fantastically costumed players. The reason why we do not need any stage director or prompter is perhaps simply because the property man is sure to place the chair properly when the player ought to sit down, and to provide a cushion when he or she ought to kneel. In the case when a hero is to die an heroic death he can fall down majestically and steadily, for the never-failing hands of the property man are always on the watch and will promptly catch him before any disaster can take place. Nevertheless, this excellent master of ceremonies sometimes in an excess of zeal overdoes his duty by even looking after the personal wants and worldly comforts of the players! For instance, when a player has some long lines to recite, or has just finished a speech, he quietly presents to him or her a cup of tea to ease the throat. In hot weather, when the costume is rather thick, he fans the wearer incessantly. These actions would certainly be condemned by a Western audience, but we accept, or rather pretend not to see, them. There is, at least, this advantage. If some accidental mistake happens to the player or property, he can come forward and put it right before the audience can decide whether it is part of the play or not, whereas on a Western stage this would be impossible!

In this play I have not attempted in the least to alter anything. The following pages present a typical play exactly as produced on a Chinese stage. It is every inch a Chinese play except the language, which, as far as my very limited English allows, I have interpreted as satisfactorily as I can.

In conclusion, I must confess that though I have translated and written a few books for the Chinese public, this is my first attempt at producing anything in a language that is not my mother-tongue, and I hope the public will view it with the gracious indulgence usually granted to foreign writers.

S. I. HSIUNG

LONDON
March 1934

LADY PRECIOUS STREAM

THE first production of the play took place at the Little Theatre, Strand, London, W.C.2, on Tuesday, November 27th, 1934, and it was presented by the People's National Theatre with the following cast:

HIS EXCELLENCY WANG YUN, the Prime Minister .	ESME PERCY
MADAM WANG, of the Chen Family, his Wife .	LOUISE HAMPTON
SU, THE DRAGON GENERAL, their Eldest Son-in-law .	ANDREW LEIGH
WEI, THE TIGER GENERAL, their Second Son-in-law	MORRIS HARVEY
GOLDEN STREAM, their Eldest Daughter, Su's Wife .	MARY CASSON
SILVER STREAM, their Second Daughter, Wei's Wife .	VERA LENNOX
PRECIOUS STREAM, their Third Daughter . .	. MAISIE DARRELL
HER MAID	AMY DALBY
HSIEH PING-KUEI, THEIR GARDENER . . .	ROGER LIVESEY
SUITORS	DAVID LEWIS, DOUGLAS ALLEN JAMES PENSTONE, ROBERT SYERS
DRIVER	. WILLIAM BELL
HER ROYAL HIGHNESS, the PRINCESS OF THE WESTERN REGIONS	FABIA DRAKE
MA TA KIANG HAI } HER A.D.C.s . . .	MAXWELL REYNOLDS MICHAEL OSLER
HER MAIDS	JANE FEY, ELINOR POWELL CANDIDA JOHN, BETTY ANDERSON
MU	. ANDREW LEIGH
WARDEN	. JACK TWYMAN
EXECUTIONER	GEOFFREY WILKINSON
HIS EXCELLENCY THE MINISTER OF FOREIGN AFFAIRS .	JACK TWYMAN
PROPERTY MEN . . .	RAYMOND FARRELL, THOMAS CLARKSON
CHINESE ATTENDANTS, WESTERN ATTENDANTS, SOLDIERS, ETC.	
HONOURABLE READER	HAROLD WARRENDER

Play produced by NANCY PRICE and S. I. HSIUNG

LADY PRECIOUS STREAM

OPENING ROUTINE: STAGE LIGHTS *set on dim marks.* HOUSE LIGHTS *out.* BLUE FOOTLIGHTS *on.* *When* HOUSE LIGHTS *out,* GONG NO. I. READER *enter between curtains to in front of curtain.* SPOT *on* READER.

READER (*to audience*). Good evening (afternoon), ladies and gentlemen. You are now introduced to the traditional Chinese stage, which, according to our humble convention, is not in the least realistic. Scenery is a thing we have never heard of, and the property men who are supposed to be unseen by the audience, are taking an active part in the performance. The success or failure of a production is sometimes in their hands. They provide chairs for the actors to sit on and cushions for them to kneel upon; and when the hero is to die an heroic death he can fall down majestically and without any hesitation, for the never-failing hands of the property men are always on the watch and will promptly catch him before any disaster can take place. Nevertheless they sometimes, in an excess of zeal, overdo their duty by even looking after the worldly comforts of the players. When the actor has just finished some long lines, they would present him with a cup of tea to ease the throat. These actions would certainly be condemned by a western audience but we accept or rather pretend not to see them. There is, at least, one advantage; if some accident happens to the actor or property they can come forward and put it right before the audience can decide whether it is part of the play or not.

(GONG NO. 2—*curtain up.*)

Now let us imagine that this unfurnished stage represents the scene of the picturesque garden of the Prime Minister, Wang Yun, who appears wearing a long black beard which indicates that he is not the villain of the piece. In spite of his very long beard, His Excellency is a middle-aged man who has always found life easy and happy. As he is a man of peppery temper he is sometimes cross when he has really nothing to find fault with. He is a strict master of his home, which he rules with an iron hand, though his wife says that he should have some one at his elbow. In Government he finds that to rule a nation is much easier than to rule a family. That is, no doubt, why we have so many prominent statesmen in history.

Madame, his wife, is a kind lady of uncertain age. To her children she seems to be more than a hundred, while to her husband she is but a mere child. She is one of the women who know the importance of the ancient female virtues. To obey your father when young, to obey your husband when married, and to obey your children when a mother. By obeying people all her life she has acquired a benign look and a soft voice.

Their eldest son-in-law, Su, the Dragon General, is a famous warrior because he always wins the battle when the enemy's General knows less about making war than he does. He knows nothing, but enough to be aware of his own ignorance.

Their second son-in-law, Wei, the Tiger General, is also a famous warrior because he always has the best of luck though it would be impossible to find a worse soldier. He knows nothing and does less, but he talks endlessly and has consequently become famous.

As for the daughters of the family, they are such charming young ladies that the author finds his English inadequate to describe their charms. However, charming ladies need no introduction—but we must warn you against Lady Precious Stream, our heroine, because she could make you put the halter willingly around your neck—if she chose to lead you along with her.

The hero of the piece, Hsieh Ping-Kuei, gardener to

His Excellency, is a man of deeds rather than words. So it would not do him justice if we vainly try to describe his merits, which, we hope, will prevent him from putting that halter willingly around his own neck.

(READER *bows and exits D.L.*)

ACT I

GONG NO. 3—STAGE LIGHTS *up.* PROPERTY MEN *enter L. and R. and bow to audience—sit at their places.* GONG NO. 4 —MUSIC. *Enter* 1ST *and* 2ND ATTENDANTS *from R. They go downstage R.* 1ST ATTENDANT *crosses front of stage to D.L.* 2ND ATTENDANT *stays D.R.* WANG *follows* ATTENDANTS *on, going D.C. Bows to audience.* PROPERTY MAN L. *brings on table and places it D.L. As* WANG *starts to speak* MUSIC *stops.*

WANG. I am your humble servant, Wang Yun, the Prime Minister of the Emperor's Court. My consort's name is Chen. Although we have been happily married for twenty years, we are still childless. It is true that we have three daughters but that doesn't count; as you know, daughters leave their parents and become other people's property. My eldest daughter is called Golden Stream, who married Su, the Dragon General; the second is called Silver Stream, who married Wei, the Tiger General. The one dearest to my heart is the youngest, called Precious Stream— (PROPERTY MAN R. *places arm-chair C.*)—who will be sixteen next February. I have a mind to choose for her amongst the rich and young nobles for a son-in-law, but the little minx is as wilful as she is pretty, and refuses to obey my wishes.

(ATTENDANTS *come to C. Pantomime opening large double door. They return to D.L. and D.R.*)

(WANG *enters garden, stepping over threshold, and sits C.*)

However, to-day's New Year's day; I will spread a feast here in my garden and have all my family present, and let my wife, my two sons-in-law and my two elder daughters try to persuade her to come to reason. Attendants!

ATTENDANTS (*kneeling*).   Yes, Excellency!

WANG.   Request Madam to come here.

ATTENDANTS (*rising*).   Yes, Excellency.

> (*They go U.R. and U.L., face off R. and call.*)

His Excellency requests the presence of Madam.

MADAM (*off R.*).   Yes, I will come.

> (MUSIC *starts.* 1ST *and* 2ND MAIDS *enter from R. Go D.S. to D.R.,* 1ST MAID *crosses front to D.L.,* 2ND MAID *stays D.R.* MADAM *follows them in to D.C. Curtsies to audience.* ATTENDANTS *return to D.L. and D.R.* MUSIC *stops*).

I am Chen, the wife of the Prime Minister, Wang.

> (*She turns U.S., steps over threshold, curtsies to* WANG.)

My respects to Your Excellency.

> (PROPERTY MAN L. *places arm-chair L. of* WANG.)

WANG.   And mine to you.   Be seated.

> (*She sits L. of* WANG.   MAIDS *cross to D.C. Step over threshold,* 1ST MAID *goes L,* 2ND MAID *goes R. to stand over* MADAM'S *chair.*)

MADAM.   May I know what is your wish in asking me to come to see you in the garden?

WANG.   To-day is New Year's Day.   I want to celebrate it in some way.   It looks as if it is going to snow. I propose that we have a feast here in the garden to enjoy the snow.   And during the feast I hope you will try your best to persuade our youngest daughter to consent to marry one of the young nobles whose suit I have approved.

MADAM.   Your orders will be obeyed.   But I am afraid it will not be of any use, for the young minx is very obstinate.   She insists on being allowed to choose for herself.

WANG. Nonsense! It is scandalous for a young girl to choose a husband herself. Our young generation is becoming hopeless. What are the teachings of Confucius and Mencius coming to? They study them and then act in defiance of them.

(*He shows a trifle of anger.*)

MADAM. She says that 'Not to impose your will upon others' is one of the most important teachings of Confucius and she hopes you will not forget it.

WANG (*blowing his long beard in a rage*). Ph-ew! You have utterly spoiled her. For heaven's sake do not encourage her to rebel against me.

(*He turns aside and calls.*)

Attendants!

ATTENDANTS (*kneeling*). Yes, Excellency!

WANG. Tell General Su, General Wei, and the ladies to come here at once.

ATTENDANTS. Yes, Excellency!

(*They rise—cross upstage R. and L. and call aloud.*)

His Excellency asks General Su and General Wei and his three daughters to come to see him.

VOICES. Yes, we are coming.

(MUSIC *starts.* MADAM *receives cup of tea from* PROPERTY MAN L., *gives it to* WANG *who drinks and returns cup to* MADAM. *She returns it to* PROPERTY MAN, *who retires to his place. During the above business* SU *has entered followed by* WEI. SU *to* D.L.C. WEI *to* D.R.C. *Both face audience.* MUSIC *stops.*)

SU (*bows*). Your humble servant Su, the Dragon General

WEI (*bows*). Wei, the Tiger General, at your service.

(PROPERTY MAN R. *places two chairs R. of* WANG.)

SU (*they face each other*). Just a moment ago our father-in-law, the Prime Minister, asked us to come to the garden to see him. I wonder what is the reason.

WEI. So do I. Let us go up and find out. (*Bows.*)

SU (*stretching out his R. arm. Bows*). You first.

(*They enter together and bow to* WANG.)

SU and WEI (*bowing*). Your sons-in-law beg to pay their respects to you.

WANG and MADAM. Don't stand on ceremony, but please be seated.

SU and WEI. Thank you!

(MUSIC *starts. They move R., bow to each other, sit,* SU *next to* WANG; WEI *R. of* SU. GOLDEN STREAM *and* SILVER STREAM *enter R. They pause at entrance and bus. of arranging hair. They come down C. curtsy to audience.* MUSIC *stops.*)

GOLDEN S. (*L.C. to audience*). Your humble maid, Golden Stream, the eldest daughter of the Wang family. My husband is Su, the Dragon General.

(PROPERTY MAN L. *places two chairs L. of* MADAM.)

SILVER S. (*R.C. to audience*). The second daughter, Silver Stream, at your service. My husband is Wei, the Tiger General, and the most handsome man in the kingdom. When we were talking in the reception room our father called us to come here.

(*She peeps over her shoulder, looking right and left.*)

It seems there is going to be a family council, and I believe I know the reason why.

(*The* TWO SISTERS *now face each other.*)

My eldest sister. (*Curtsy.*)

GOLDEN STREAM. Yes, my youngest sister. (*Curtsy.*)

SILVER S. Do you know why father has called us to come here?

GOLDEN S. No, I don't know.

SILVER S. (*speaking very rapidly*). Because of our minx of a sister. I'm sure it's about her . . . She is not very young now and she is choosing a husband for herself. No wonder, I would do the same if I were in her place. But Father is also choosing one for her, and no wonder, I would do the same if I were in his place. And Mother——

GOLDEN S. (*interrupting her*). All right, don't talk so much. Let us go in.

(*They enter up to* WANG *and* MADAM, *curtsy.*)

GOLDEN S. and SILVER S. (*together*). Your daughters have come to pay their respects to you, dear father and mother.

WANG and MADAM. Don't stand on ceremony. Be seated.

GOLDEN S. and SILVER S. Thank you.

(*They both sit,* GOLDEN STREAM *next to* MADAM, SILVER STREAM *L. of* GOLDEN STREAM.)

SILVER S. (*quick and sharp.*) Are you calling us here to discuss the case of my youngest sister, Precious Stream?

WANG. Eh—yes; no, not exactly. To-day is New Year's Day. I want to celebrate it in some way. It looks as if it is going to snow. I propose that we have a feast here in the garden to enjoy the snow. And during the feast, well——

SILVER S. Oh, I know! And during the feast we will try our best to persuade our youngest sister to consent to marry one of the young nobles whose suit you have approved. Isn't that so?

WANG. Yes, that is exactly what I wish you to do.

GOLDEN S. But if she has a suitor in her own mind——

WANG. Nonsense, I won't allow it.

GOLDEN S. Is that fair, dear father?

MADAM. Yes, is that fair, dear?

WANG. Well—a daughter's duty is to obey.

SILVER S. Father knows everything of consequence, and if our youngest sister's secret suitor is a desirable person, then he must be on father's list. Otherwise, it must be some unsuitable creature whom it would be well and proper to avoid. When I was young I left my

choice entirely in dear father's hands, and, you see,
I became the wife of the most handsome man in the
kingdom.

(Rises, curtsies, and sits.)

WEI. Oh, I thank you.

(Hides face with sleeve.)

GOLDEN S. *(sarcastically).* But father can't find another
man as handsome as your husband for her now.

WEI. Yes, that's true.

SILVER S. Not another word, please, she is coming.

(MUSIC starts. PROPERTY MAN L. *places chair L. for*
PRECIOUS STREAM. PRECIOUS STREAM *enters preceded by*
MAID. MAID *to L.C.,* PRECIOUS STREAM *does bus. of
arranging hair, then down to C.* MUSIC *stops.)*

PRECIOUS S. I am your humble maid, Precious Stream,
the third and youngest daughter of the Wang family.
When I was doing my embroidery work in my boudoir,
I heard my father calling to me to come to the garden
to see him. My maid, lead the way to the garden.

MAID. Yes, my lady.

(MAID enters the garden and goes L. followed by PRECIOUS
STREAM. PRECIOUS STREAM *up C to* WANG, *curtsies.)*

PRECIOUS S. Your daughter's respects to you, dear father
and mother.

WANG and MADAM. Don't stand on ceremony, be seated.

PRECIOUS S. Thank you. And my compliments to my
brothers-in-law and my dear sisters.

(Sits L., 3RD MAID *crosses behind* PRECIOUS STREAM'S
chair. ATTENDANTS *close door and cross U.R. to behind
chairs.)*

ALL. Thank you. The same to you.

PRECIOUS S. May I know why I am called to come
here, dear father?

WANG. Yes. Ahem! Well—the fact is, eh—to-day—eh
—to-day is—eh——

(At this point the stage picture is):

C

2ND   2ND and 1ST   3RD   1ST
ATTENDANT   MAIDS   MAID   ATTENDANT
WEI—SU—WANG—MADAM—GOLD. S.—SIL. S.—PREC. S.

C

SILVER S. Allow me, father. *(Rapidly as if reciting a poem.)*
To-day is New Year's Day. Father wants to celebrate
it in some way. It looks as if it is going to snow.
Father proposes that we have a feast here in the garden
to enjoy the snow. And during the feast he wishes——

WANG *(uneasily)*. Ahem!—Ahem! That will do, thank
you.

PRECIOUS S. Splendid. Call the servants to arrange
the table at once. And when the snow is falling we
shall have the gentlemen to write poems for the occasion.
I think my brothers-in-law will be glad to do so.

SU and WEI *(looking at each other and shaking heads)*. No.

WANG. Attendants!

      (ATTENDANTS downstage R. and L. and kneel.)

ATTENDANTS. Yes, Excellency.

WANG. Remove that big rock to the centre, and let it
serve as our table.

                  (Points to table D.L.)

ATTENDANTS. Yes, Excellency.

      *(They go to table L. one above and one below it. They
      try to lift it, pause, take breath, try again, but are unable
      to move it. Kneel.)*

Excellency, the rock refuses to be moved!

WANG. Nonsense! What useless creatures you are!

      *(ATTENDANTS cross U.L., returning to places, U.L. and
      U.R.)*

MADAM. But, my dear, it is too heavy for them.

WEI. Cowards! If it refuses to be moved why don't
you kick it.

SILVER S. Yes, why don't you kick it?

PRECIOUS S. Dear father, I do think it's too heavy for them. Why don't you ask my brothers-in-law to remove it? They are renowned all the world over for their strength. It would be real sport.

WEI. My dear relative, as our greatest sage Confucius said: 'To kill a little chicken, why use a big knife which is made for killing horses!'

WANG (*correcting him*). '. . . for killing oxen' is the ancient text.

WEI. So, to lift this little rock is too small a feat for me, it is also beneath my dignity. If there were a big rock, say ten times as large as that, or even larger, then I would do it with pleasure, and with great ease, I assure you.

SILVER S. Yes, I can assure you, too.

SU (*a more truthful and practical man*). As none of us can remove that rock, may I make a suggestion?

WANG. Certainly.

ALL. Yes.

SU. You know the gardener, Hsieh Ping-Kuei, before coming into our service was a street acrobat. I remember having seen him perform wonderful feats of strength by lifting up huge stones, now I . . .

WEI. Yes, I saw him lifting up a stone ten times as big as that one. Order him to remove it for us.

SILVER S. Yes, order him to do it.

PRECIOUS S. Then don't you think this rock is too small for him?

WANG. Attendants!

(ATTENDANTS *down L. and R. kneel.*)

ATTENDANTS. Yes, Excellency.

WANG. Order the gardener, Hsieh Ping-Kuei, to come here at once.

ATTENDANTS. Yes, Excellency.

(*Both go up L. and R. and call off L.*)

His Excellency orders the gardener, Hsieh Ping-Kuei, to come here at once.

HSIEH (*off stage*). His Excellency's orders will be obeyed.

(ATTENDANTS *move to their places L. and R. behind chairs.* HSIEH *enters L., gets book from* PROPERTY MAN. *Down to C., addresses audience.*)

HSIEH. I am your humble servant, Hsieh Ping-Kuei, once a beggar, now the gardener to His Excellency the Prime Minister Wang. There is very little work to be done here, so I am always reading, hoping to make up the time I wasted in my youth. I hear that His Excellency is calling me. Let me go inside and see what are his orders.

(*He puts down his back, the book. Enters garden and kneels before* WANG, *R.C.*)

Your humble gardener, Hsieh Ping-Kuei, begs to report himself for your Excellency's orders.

WANG. I want you to remove that rock to the centre.

MADAM. It will serve as a table, you see.

HSIEH. Very well, your Excellency.

(*He goes to table, picks it up, raises it up L. and behind row of chairs. He stumbles and almost falls.*)

ALL (*startled*). Oooooooooooo——

(HSIEH *brings table to in front of* WANG *at C.*)

HSIEH. Is that all right, your Excellency?

WANG. All right, you may go now.

(HSIEH *crosses L., as he passes* PRECIOUS STREAM.)

PRECIOUS S. All of us, and especially General Wei thank you very much.

(HSIEH *bows.*)

That will do, you may go now.

(*He goes off L.*)

WEI. That's nothing. I can easily remove a rock ten times larger.

WANG. Attendants!

ATTENDANTS (*coming D.L. and D.R., kneeling*). Yes, Excellency.

WANG. Serve the feast here.

                 (MUSIC *starts.*)

ATTENDANTS (*rising*). Yes, Excellency.

     (PROPERTY MAN R. *gives tray with wine jug and seven cups on it to* ATTENDANT R. (*2nd*), *who carries it C. gives it to* ATTENDANT L., *who puts it on table, before* WANG.)

WANG (*rising.* MUSIC *softer*). Precious Stream, my dear daughter, serve the wine.

     (MUSIC *louder.* PRECIOUS STREAM *pours wine.* MUSIC *softer.*)

Madam, my honourable sons-in-law, my dear daughters, please drink.

     (MUSIC *louder. As he names them, they come forward to table and pick up wine cups together.*)

ALL. Thank you.

           (*They drink.* MUSIC *softer.*)

WANG. The wine is excellent. Now once more.

     (MUSIC *louder.* PRECIOUS STREAM *repeats pouring business.*)

ALL. Thank you.

     (*They drink. As they are drinking, the* PROPERTY MEN *bring chairs D.L. and D.R., face centre standing on chairs, unfurl flags and allow snow to fall, then return chairs and retire to their places.* MUSIC *stops.*)

WANG. What a beautiful scene the snow makes.

                 (ALL *sit.*)

Having wine and snow, we must also have some poems to celebrate the occasion. Who is going to write them?

(*Looks to sons-in-law.* PROPERTY MAN R. *takes away wine jug and tray*—PROPERTY MAN L. *takes away table.*)

SU. I am a very poor scholar, my dear father-in-law, and I must ask you to excuse me.

GOLDEN S. Father will, of course, excuse you.

WEI. Although I am known as the most brilliant scholar, my dear father-in-law, I regret to say that I am not in the right mood for poetry now. I remember some poet said: 'To write good poems, one needs inspiration!' It is very cold now, you see. We can't expect any perspiration until summer comes.

(ALL *except* WANG *and* SILVER STREAM *smile.* SILVER STREAM *is upset.*)

WANG. Perspiration? You mean inspiration.

PRECIOUS S. If it's only perspiration you need, then you must be the greatest poet of the age!

WEI. Oh, thank you.

SILVER S. For shame to chaff my dear one like this.

SU. As none of us can write any poetry, may I make another suggestion?

ALL. Yes.

WANG. Certainly.

SU. I remember having heard the gardener, Hsieh Ping-Kuei, sing beautiful songs in the street, and I was told they were composed by himself.

GOLDEN S. Yes, I remember, too.

WEI. No, I don't think he composed them.

WANG. Yes, he did, and that's why I took a fancy to him, and gave him the post of my gardener, as a just reward for his talent.

WEI. Truly, you are the most just Prime Minister in history. Now let him repay some of your kindness by entertaining us with his songs.

SILVER S. Yes, if he really can.

WANG.   Attendants!

ATTENDANTS.   Yes, Excellency.

(*They come down L. and R. and kneel.*)

WANG.   Order the gardener, Hsieh Ping-Kuei, to come here again.

ATTENDANTS.   Yes, Excellency.

(*Go up L. and R.   Call off L.*)

His Excellency orders the gardener, Hsieh Ping-Kuei, to come here again.

HSIEH (*off stage*).   Coming.

(ATTENDANTS *retire to their places.*   HSIEH *enters L., returns book to* PROPERTY MAN *and comes to below* PRECIOUS STREAM's *chair, and kneels.*)

WANG.   As we are drinking wine and enjoying the snow here, we find we need a little poem to celebrate the occasion.   As I have heard that you are somewhat of a poet in your own way, I order you to give us one of your poems.

HSIEH.   If Your Excellency will excuse my being forward——

WANG.   Certainly.

HSIEH.   I must beg to point out to Your Excellency that I am one of your labourers and my duty to Your Excellency is limited to labour.

WEI.   Bravo!   I said he couldn't!

SILVER S.   So did I.

SU.   Wait a moment—what do you mean?

GOLDEN S.   Tell us candidly.

HSIEH.   If it is not my labour but my talent you want, then I must beg you to treat me as a gentleman and I must be invited, not ordered.

WEI.   Impossible!   What impudence!

SILVER S.   The man ought to be thrashed.

PRECIOUS S.   Why this is most reasonable.   A true poet

must not be treated as a workman. Why shouldn't
we treat him with proper respect?

WANG. Well, to show that I am a just man I will give
you a seat in that corner, and request you to write a
short poem of four lines on the subject of 'Wine, Snow
and Poetry.' If your poem proves to be good, I will
give you a reward; if your poem is bad, or you can't
write at all——

WEI. I'll have him punished for his impudence!

SILVER S. That's exactly my view.

WANG. Do you hear, man?

HSIEH. Yes, your Excellency.

    (*He rises, crosses to D.L. and calls.*)

Attendants, bring me pen, inkstone and paper!

WEI. What insolence!

WANG. Really, this is too much!

    (PROPERTY MAN L. *gives pen, inkstone and paper on tray
to* PRECIOUS STREAM'S (3RD) MAID.)

PRECIOUS S Why, this is but the true attitude of a poet.
If no one will bring you what you want, allow me.

    (MUSIC *starts.* PRECIOUS STREAM *rises and goes to* HSIEH,
MAID *follows* to PRECIOUS STREAM'S *R.* PROPERTY MAN
L. *brings* PRECIOUS STREAM'S *chair to* HSIEH. *He sits.*
PRECIOUS STREAM *prepares ink on inkstone, points the pen,
hands paper to* HSIEH, *gives him prepared pen. She gets
behind chair.* MAID *to her L.* MUSIC *stops.*)

HSIEH (*as he writes*). 'Wine brings a double cheer if snow
be here.'

WANG. 'Wine brings a double cheer if snow be here.'

HSIEH. 'Snow takes a brighter white from song's delight.'

WANG. 'Snow takes a brighter white from song's delight.'

HSIEH. 'Ah, but when cups abound, and song is sweet,
And snow is falling 'round, the joy's complete.'

WANG. '. . . the joy's complete.'

(While this is being written, all nod their heads in time to the rhythm, with the exception of WEI. PRECIOUS STREAM *takes back pen, gives it to* MAID—*returns to her place.* MAID *follows.* HSIEH *rises, crosses to* WANG. PROPERTY MAN L. *brings back* PRECIOUS STREAM'S *chair and takes tray from* MAID.)

HSIEH. Here you are, your Excellency.

(Hands him the paper and backs to D.L.)

WANG. Well, it is very good indeed.

(Passes paper to SU.)

SU. Yes, very good.

(Tries to pass paper to WEI.)

WEI. I don't think so. I could write a much better poem.

SILVER S. Yes, I'm sure you could.

WANG *(to* HSIEH). Thank you. You may go now. A reward will be given to you—later on.

MADAM. I will order the steward to give it to you.

HSIEH *(bowing)*. Many thanks, your Excellency.

(Starts to leave.)

WANG *(to his wife)*. You see, my dear, our family needs a poet.

(At this point, HSIEH *stops, bows to* PRECIOUS STREAM. WANG *sees and is indignant.* HSIEH *exits L.)*

When we want to celebrate an occasion like this we find that none of our family can write anything. Now those suitors whom I have approved all write first-class poems. All the poems they have *shown* to me are excellent.

PRECIOUS S. My brother-in-law Wei also used to show you very good poems before he married my sister.

WEI. I can still show you good poems if I am allowed.

SILVER S. Yes, I am sure he can.

PRECIOUS S. I should like to see you write them in my presence.

WEI. Impossible!

SILVER S. Imposs——

(*All snicker.*)

WANG. How unreasonable. But these young suitors are also all rich and of high birth; indeed, one couldn't find any one better than they are in every way.

PRECIOUS S. May I ask you, dear father, is every one of them rich and noble?

WANG. Yes, certainly.

PRECIOUS S. Are there not one or two among them not so rich and noble?

WANG. No. None. They are all equally rich and equally noble.

PRECIOUS S. (*rises and curtsies*). Then, dear father, how can I choose? By choosing one, it will be unfair to the others. To be fair, I think I must refuse them all.

(*She sits.*)

WANG. Oh!

(*He puts his hand to his forehead.*)

MADAM (*laughs*). You have outwitted your father, dear child.

GOLDEN S. Very clever, indeed.

SILVER S. Very silly.

PRECIOUS S. (*coaxingly*). Dear father, you are the Prime Minister and therefore the most clever man in the kingdom!

(WANG *is rather flattered and looks pleased.*)

When the most clever man in the kingdom is at a loss as to say who is the most suitable, then how can I, a stupid young girl without any experience, make a decision?

MADAM. That's true.

GOLDEN S. Yes, dear father, it's quite true.

SILVER S. No! When I was young I was neither stupid nor without experience.

(ALL *react.*)

WEI. Why don't you refer the matter to the imperial counsellors, so that they may hold a conference?

SU. Nonsense! Our dear father-in-law will settle it sooner or later. In the meantime, let us drop it.

PRECIOUS S. (*she rises, curtsies*). Thank you, dear brother-in-law.

(*Sits. SU smiles at her, rises and bows*).

WANG (*rises*). I think I have a very good plan for settling it.

ALL. Marvellous! How clever! So soon!

WANG. Listen, my dear. On your birthday, the second of February, there will be a festival. Let us build a beautiful pavilion here in the garden, and let all the suitors come beneath it. You, in the pavilion, take an embroidered ball and throw it down from the pavilion. The one who catches it will be your bridegroom.

PRECIOUS S. Is that a wise way to settle such a problem?

WANG. It is the only way. And I am quite determined.

(*Sits.*)

MADAM. It is romantic too!

ALL. Yes, very romantic.

PRECIOUS S. When even careful judgment is not sufficient to settle such a problem, is it wise to settle it by lottery?

WANG. It will not be a lottery. It will be the will of God.

WEI. The suitor who is hit by the embroidered ball can well call his case one of *force majeure*.

(*He laughs. SILVER STREAM laughs also. MADAM looks at WEI, who stops. Then at SILVER STREAM, who also stops laughing.*)

MADAM. I see! Whenever we find a situation which

cannot be dealt with by mortals we ask the help of God. We always turn to God when we are in distress.

ALL (*raise R. hand, fingers close together, tip of first touching mouth. Thumb to face and little finger farthest away and say*): 'La, Mo, Cho, Me, To Fu.'

MADAM. Well, now that we have put our responsibility upon God, shall we retire?

WANG. Yes, let us retire.

(MUSIC *starts.* ATTENDANTS *open doors and stand aside.* ALL *rise.* WANG *down C. followed by* MADAM. *He bows to audience and goes off L.; she curtsies and follows him, then the* TWO MAIDS *follow her.* ALL *step over threshold as on entering. As family moves downstage,* PROPERTY MEN R. *and* L. *place chairs R. and L. in their original places.* MUSIC *softer*).

SU. We have some business at my house if you will excuse us.

(*He and* GOLDEN STREAM *bow and curtsy to audience and exit L.—he first, she following him.* WEI *crosses to* PRECIOUS STREAM.)

WEI. Now, dear sister-in-law, allow me to give you a little advice.

PRECIOUS S. (*pointing out to audience*). Look, there is a rock ten times as large as the one used for our table. I think you said a moment ago you could lift such a rock with ease. Now, will you please——

(SILVER STREAM *to L. of him, pulls his sleeve.*)

WEI. I think we have some important business waiting for us, too. Good morning.

(MUSIC *louder.* WEI *and* SILVER STREAM *down C. bow and curtsy to audience and exit L.* ATTENDANTS *follow them and close doors of garden, exit L.* PROPERTY MAN L. *places chair C.* MUSIC *stops.*)

PRECIOUS S. (*goes R.*). What *shall* I do?

(*Goes L.*)

What shall I do?

(*Taps her forehead, then up centre, sits.*)

My maid—ask the gardener Hsieh Ping-Kuei to come to me.

MAID.　Yes, my lady.

　　　　　(*To upstage L. and calls.*)

Lady Precious Stream wishes the gardener, Hsieh Ping-Kuei, to come here immediately.

HSIEH (*offstage*).　Yes, I am coming.

　　　　　(MAID *to* L. *of* PRECIOUS STREAM.　HSIEH *enters and kneels* L. *before* PRECIOUS STREAM.)

May I know your orders, my lady?

PRECIOUS S.　Stand up, please.

　　　　　(*He rises.*)

My maid.　Provide a seat for Mr. Hsieh.

　　　　　(PROPERTY MAN L. *places chair behind* HSIEH.)

HSIEH.　How can I sit down before you, my lady.

PRECIOUS S.　The best of manners is obedience.

HSIEH (*bows and sits*).　Then I must thank you.

PRECIOUS S.　My maid.　Go to my boudoir and fetch some fifty taels of silver for me.

　　　　　(MAID *curtsies and goes down* C.)

Go as quickly as possible.

　　　　　(MAID *opens door, goes* C. *closes door and stoops as if listening.*　PRECIOUS STREAM *comes down* C. *opens the door and says*)

And return as slowly as possible.

　　　　　(MAID *jumps up, moves* L. *and says*)

MAID.　Yes, my lady.

　　　　　(*Exits L.*)

PRECIOUS S. (*returns and sits*).　Mr. Hsieh, I now know that you are a man of both high literary and military abilities.　I wish to help you, but first of all you must tell me about your family.

HSIEH.　Thank you, my lady.　Do you really want to know about my family?　Well, I am of a very poor family.

PRECIOUS S. That I know. I want to hear about the members of your family.

HSIEH. My father and mother are both dead.

PRECIOUS S. I see. Is there any one else in your family?

HSIEH. Being poor, I only had one father and one mother!

PRECIOUS S. I mean those of your own generation.

HSIEH. I had a brother who died at five. I have no sister.

PRECIOUS S. Did any one of your family marry?

HSIEH. Yes.

PRECIOUS S. (*taken aback*). Oh! Who?

HSIEH. Well, my father married my mother.

PRECIOUS S. (*relieved*). Of course! And your brother?

HSIEH. As he died at five he did not marry.

PRECIOUS S. I see. Well—and did—did your parents have a daughter-in-law at all?

HSIEH. No, they had none.

PRECIOUS S. Then I have something to tell you, but I find it hard to do so. *Well*, do you understand riddles?

HSIEH. A little.

PRECIOUS S. On the second of February it will be my sixteenth birthday, and I am going to marry the man who is hit by the embroidered ball which I shall throw down from a beautiful pavilion to be erected here. It will be a case of the will of God, but I have resolved to take it into my own hands. I have in mind a suitable person. Now, this person, if you look far——

(*Pointing away into the distance.*)

HSIEH (*continuing her speech*). . . . is a thousand miles away——

PRECIOUS S. Yes, and if you look near——

(*Pointing near to her.*)

HSIEH. Then he is before you!

(*Rises.*)

PRECIOUS S. Thank you! That is exactly what I mean.

(MAID *enters R. comes downstage, takes silver from* PROPERTY MAN R.)

HSIEH. If my lady bestows on me such an honour I will never fail her!

PRECIOUS S. My maid is returning. Not another word. Be sure to be present on the second of February.

(MAID *opens door.*)

HSIEH. The second of February.

MAID (*up to R. of* PRECIOUS STREAM). Here you are, my lady.

PRECIOUS S. Give it to Mr. Hsieh.

(MAID *crosses to* HSIEH *and gives him the piece of silver, then stands U.L. of* PRECIOUS STREAM.)

HSIEH. Thank you. I shall never forget your kindness.
(*Down C.*)

The second of February.

(*Goes up L. gives* PROPERTY MAN *the piece of silver and exits.*)

PRECIOUS S. (*rises*). Let's retire to our boudoir and wait for the will of God.

(*Exits L.*)

MAID NO. 3. (*crosses D.C. to audience*). The Will of God.

(MUSIC *starts.* MAID *laughs, moves U.L. laughing as she exits.* MUSIC *stops.* LIGHTS *fade.* LIGHTS *up immediately after they have come down.* MUSIC *starts. Enter* ATTENDANTS, *followed by* WANG. ATTENDANTS *cross to D.R. and D.L.,* WANG *TO D.C.*)

WANG. To-day *is* the second of February, the day on which I am going to take a new son-in-law into my family.

(*Crosses U.C. and sits.*)

(*During the exit of the* MAID *and the entrance of* WANG *the* PROPERTY MAN L. *places the two chairs L.C. and R.C. with*

backs to audience. PROPERTY MAN R. *places arm-chair C.
for* WANG. PROPERTY MAN L. *goes off L. and returns with
table which he places between the L.C. and R.C. chairs.*
PROPERTY MAN R. *goes off R. and brings on embroidery
attached to bamboo sticks. This he and* PROPERTY MAN L.
tie to outside of the two chairs.)

WANG. I have been looking forward to it enormously,
and I am very happy to find the weather is so fine. It
is now quite near the hour of throwing the ball, and
I must give the necessary instructions. Attendants!

ATTENDANTS (*kneeling*). Yes, Excellency.

WANG. You must stay in the garden and guard the gate.
Admit only those young gentlemen you know I like.

(*Enter* FOUR SUITORS *from R.—*IST *and* 2ND *to D.L.C.*
3RD *and* 4TH *to D.R.C.*)

As soon as the embroidered ball has been thrown I will
come back at once.

ATTENDANTS (*rising*). Yes, Excellency.

IST SUITOR (*to audience, bowing*). Lady Precious Stream
is as beautiful as the flowers of May.

2ND SUITOR (*same business*). The second of February is
her wedding day.

3RD SUITOR (*same business*). The young suitors come here
happy and gay!

4TH SUITOR (*same business*). Who will be the lucky one——

WANG (*rises*). Nobody can say.

(*He exits L.* PROPERTY MAN R. *removes arm-chair
from C.*)

IST SUITOR. Here we have arrived. Let us knock at
the gate.

(*They turn and knock at gate.*)

IST ATTENDANT. Yes, I am coming.

(*He opens the door, coming C. with* 2ND ATTENDANT.)

Good morning, my young lords. Have you young
gentlemen come to await the lucky ball?

SUITORS. Exactly.

1ST ATTENDANT. Come in, please.

(1ST ATTENDANT *shows the way to the L. round stage,
below pavilion to R., they imitating his movements.* 2ND
ATTENDANT *closes door. Both return to places D.R. and
D.L.)*

ALL. (4) Lady Precious Stream is coming.

(MUSIC *starts.* LADY PRECIOUS STREAM *enters R.* TWO
MAIDS *before and* TWO MAIDS *after her. She goes to C.,*
TWO MAIDS *R. and* TWO MAIDS *L. of her—all standing facing
her. She carries an embroidered ball, given her by* PROPERTY
MAN R. MUSIC *stops.*)

PRECIOUS S. Time flies and to-day is the fatal day of the
second of February. Although I am anxious to be
free from suspense, the idea of going up to the pavilion
and throwing down the embroidered ball while the
crowd looks on makes me feel very shy, and I don't
know how I shall ever manage to carry on. My maids!

MAIDS. Yes, my lady.

(*Curtsy.*)

PRECIOUS S. Lead the way to the pavilion, please.

MAIDS. Yes, my lady.

(*Curtsy.* MUSIC *starts. The* TWO MAIDS *L., come C.
and go round stage, below the pavilion, followed by the* TWO
MAIDS *R.* LADY PRECIOUS STREAM *follows them. They go
round stage once, then up behind pavilion.* LADY PRECIOUS
STREAM *goes in the pavilion.* MUSIC *stops.*)

PRECIOUS S. (*surveying the crowd represented by the* SUITORS).
Now I must look carefully. There are princes dressed
in red and there are young nobles dressed in blue.
(*As the colour of each* SUITOR'S *costume is mentioned he steps
out of line and then back.*) Those clad in yellow are
the sons of rich merchants, and those in white are
heirs to the great landowners! I must find where
Hsieh Ping-Kuei is standing. I have looked from east
to west, and now I must look from north to south.

Again and again I have looked for him, and nowhere is he to be seen. I remember clearly when I gave him the silver, I told him to come on this day and he promised he would. But he has proved unfaithful.

(*Then to* SUITORS, *directly.*)

Oh, woe is me! I must retire without throwing the ball.

(HSIEH *enters L. crosses D.L.*)

1ST SUITOR.   No! You musn't go back!

2ND SUITOR.   Throw the ball before you go, please!

3RD SUITOR.   How can you desert us?

4TH SUITOR.   I have been waiting all the morning!

PRECIOUS S.   Ah! I see him emerging from that corner.

(*Speaks to the* SUITORS.)

Now, gentlemen, please come near to the pavilion and listen to my words.

(SUITORS, *one step forward.*)

I want all of you to pledge your word of honour to me that you will uphold the man who, by the will of God, is going to be my husband, whoever he may be. And, moreover, that you will swear that you, one and all, will draw your swords against him who will not uphold the destined match!

ALL.   We swear!

(*Step back.*)

PRECIOUS S.   This marriage is to be arranged by the will of God, and we mortals have to abide by this arrangement. Now, catch the ball.

(*She holds ball above her head, swings it, counts.*)

One, two, three!

(SUITORS *sway and reach upward each time she counts. She throws ball and* HSIEH PING-KUEI *catches it.*)

HSIEH.   Here it is!

SUITORS.   Oh!

(*They make a move forward.*)

PRECIOUS S.   Gentlemen, remember that all of you have pledged your word of honour to me and you must abide by it.   Now, like decent folk, congratulate him and me.

ALL.   Congratulations!

HSIEH.   Thanks.

(PRECIOUS STREAM *has now got down from the pavilion. Curtsies to* HSIEH *then up to* SUITORS R. *When* PRECIOUS STREAM *gets down from pavilion,* PROPERTY MAN L. *takes table off L. returns, unties the pavilion. Takes chairs to L.* PROPERTY MAN R. *takes pavilion to R. then returns to his position R.*)

SUITORS.   Our hearty congratulations.

PRECIOUS S.   Many thanks!

(WANG *enters R. downstage to C.*)

WANG.   Where is my new son-in-law?   Where is my new son-in-law?

(*Bus. of* SUITORS *in rotation, upstage to downstage, turning back on* WANG.)

HSIEH.   At your service, my dear father-in-law.

(WANG *sees* HSIEH—*blows through beard.* PROPERTY MAN R. *brings cushion forward and catches* WANG *as he faints.* WANG *faints into the arms of* PROPERTY MEN *who lower him on to the stage.* PRECIOUS STREAM *fans him with her sleeve.*)

PRECIOUS S.   Oh, father, father!

SUITORS (*fanning* WANG *with sleeves*).   Oh, Your Excellency!   Your Excellency!

WANG (PROPERTY MEN *pick him up*).   Oh, my God!

PRECIOUS S.   Yes, dear father, this is indeed the will of God.

SUITORS (*sarcastically*).   The will of God.

WANG (*to audience*).   But I won't have it.   I will take the matter away from God into my own hands.

PRECIOUS S. But, father, aren't you glad? You said our family needed a poet, and now we have one.

      (*Crosses L. to* HSIEH.)

God has granted your wish.

WANG. We will see whether God will grant me a different wish.

PRECIOUS S. Now, my gallant suitors, did you not swear that you would draw your swords against him who dared not to uphold the destined match?

SUITORS. Yes, we did.

      (*One step forward, bravely.*)

WANG (*to* SUITORS). What!

      (SUITORS *fall back*—WANG *turns to* PRECIOUS STREAM.)

You have conspired against your own father.

PRECIOUS S. I never dreamt it would be you we should have to deal with.

WANG (*to* SUITORS). You fools, to think that I once liked you. I am a blind fool. Now get out, all of you.

      (ATTENDANTS *open doors.* HSIEH *and* PRECIOUS STREAM *go up to entrance L. and take tea from the* PROPERTY MAN. WANG *takes* SUITORS *one by one by the ear and ushers them out.*)

1ST SUITOR. Lady Precious Stream is as beautiful as the flowers in May.

2ND SUITOR. The second of February is her wedding day.

3RD SUITOR. The young suitors come here happy and gay.

4TH SUITOR. But when they are leaving they say——

WANG (*kicking* SUITOR NO. 4, *against whom* PROPERTY MAN L. *holds a cushion*). Woe is the day.

      (*They exeunt.* MUSIC *starts.* PROPERTY MAN R. *places arm-chair C.* PROPERTY MAN L. *places two chairs L. of* WANG *then* PRECIOUS STREAM'S *chair.* PROPERTY MAN R. *places two chairs R. of* WANG. WANG *sits C. Enter*

MADAM, GOLDEN STREAM, SILVER STREAM, SU *and* WEI. *They come up to* WANG, *curtsy, bow and sit.* PRECIOUS STREAM *comes down L. to her chair, does not sit.* HSIEH *goes round back, down R. and stands opposite* PRECIOUS STREAM. MUSIC *stops.*)

MADAM (*to* PRECIOUS STREAM). Why don't you sit down, my dear?

PRECIOUS S. So long as my future husband is not given a seat, I can't sit down, dear mother.

MADAM. Then be seated, both of you.

WANG. No! This is the house of a Prime Minister, not a beggar's hut. How can he be allowed to sit down here?

MADAM. Dear, you are only making the situation worse. Come, don't be headstrong. Let all of us sit down and talk over the matter, and see what is to be done.

WANG (*sulkily*). All right. Have your own way.

(PROPERTY MAN R. *places chair behind* HSIEH.)

MADAM. Now be seated, please.

(*Both sit.*)

HSIEH. Thank you, Madam.

PRECIOUS S. Thank you, dear mother.

WANG (*gruffly*). Say, man, on what conditions (MADAM *nudges him—then softly*) will you let her be free?

WEI. Allow me to arrange for you, dear father-in-law. I know how to deal with this sort of customer. Look here, my man; say, my friend! Hullo, Hsieh Ping-Kuei!

(*Rises.*)

Mr. Hsieh Ping-Kuei.

HSIEH (*fiercely*). What is your wish, my great General?

WEI. Don't be cross, my—er—Mr. Hsieh. You know it would never do for Lady Precious Stream to marry you, a beg——

(SU *nudges* WEI.)

Say—a poor man. I quite understand that this is, for you, a great chance, and that you must have a handsome price before you let go your hold.

HSIEH (*fiercely, rises*). I don't quite understand your meaning.

SILVER S. (*rises, goes R.*). You can't bully my husband. Bully him back, my dear.

(HSIEH *turns back to* WEI.)

WEI (*curtly*). Be quiet, (*softly*) dear.

(SILVER STREAM *to L. curtsies and sits.*)

I mean, that if you will let us off quietly, without any scandal, I am sure my father-in-law is willing to give you, say——

SILVER S. One hundred taels of silver.

WEI (*watching* HSIEH). No, say two hundred.

SILVER S. Not a penny more.

WANG. I am a just and generous man. I will offer you five hundred taels.

WEI. Now, be sensible, my man.

(*Sits*).

WANG. Well, how much do you want?

(MADAM *presses* WANG'S *arm.*)

How much do you want, Mr. Hsieh?

HSIEH. I want nothing from you, sir. Even millions and billions could not buy me off. The decision lies with Lady Precious Stream. If she thinks that I am not her equal, and that this is but a lamentable mistake, just let her say the word, and I will go away without taking a penny from you.

PRECIOUS S. (*rises*). Beautiful!

(HSIEH *and* PRECIOUS STREAM *sit.*)

SU. It's quite right!

MADAM. Dear, dear!

GOLDEN S.   He is playing the game!

WANG.   My dear daughter, you know that to me you are dearer than all.   Now, say the word and let us get out of this disgrace.

WEI.   And, if—eh—Mr. Hsieh actually refuses to take any money, then the five hundred taels you promised, dear father-in-law, ought to be given to me as a reward for my acting as a go-between.

SILVER S.   Of course father will reward you, dear.

PRECIOUS S. (*rises*—HSIEH *rises*).   I am sorry to deprive you of your reward.   I will stick to my match.

(HSIEH *bows.   All react.*)

To my sister (*curtsy*) I am not worth one hundred taels, and to my brother-in-law (*curtsies*) only two hundred, and even to my father (*curtsies*), who professes to love me dearer than all, I am worth only five hundred.

WANG.   No.   (*Beckons* PRECIOUS STREAM *to him.   She goes.*)   In my heart I was prepared to offer one thousand.

PRECIOUS S. (*crosses back of chair*).   Thank you, father.

(*To audience.*)

I see I am getting on.

(*To family.*)

You seem to think that one would prefer to have, let us say, a thousand taels rather than to have me.   And here is a man who refuses to take millions and billions and prefers me instead.   Shall I be so ungrateful as to give him the go-by and to remain with those who value me so little?   No, father, I decline!

(*Curtsies and sits*—HSIEH *sits.*)

GOLDEN S.   So would I!

MADAM.   Dear, dear!

SU.   Very noble.

SILVER S   Very silly!

WEI.   It's too bad.   My five hundred taels are gone.

WANG. If you insist on marrying him, all I can say is that a beggar girl is going to marry a beggar and remain one. You need not expect any dowry from me. No—not even a penny.

PRECIOUS S. (*rises*). No, father. Not a beggar girl to a beggar. But a working girl to a worker. We both can work.

WANG (*laughs*). You? Work? Impossible!

SILVER S. Don't you think it will soil your beautiful clothes?

PRECIOUS S. No, because I will not wear them.

(*She goes C. The* FAMILY *crowd round her,* MADAM *and the* TWO DAUGHTERS *L. of her, the* MEN *R. of her with back to the audience.* WANG *remains by his chair, turns his back upon them.* MADAM *helps* PRECIOUS STREAM *off with her clothes, hands them to R.* PROPERTY MAN. PRECIOUS STREAM *gives her jewels to L.* PROPERTY MAN. PROPERTY MAN R. *moves forward takes* PRECIOUS STREAM'S *dress and puts it off R.* PROPERTY MAN L. *moves forward when* PRECIOUS STREAM *receives her jewels.*) The ancient proverb says: 'A good son will not depend upon his father's wealth; and a good daughter will not depend upon her family for clothes.' Here I am giving back to you these fine clothes. And here are your jewels, too.

MADAM. Oh, dear, don't!

GOLDEN S. My poor sister.

SU. A brave girl!

SILVER S. I wonder how they will manage to live.

WEI. They will soon die of starvation.

WANG (*still in a rage*). Do you mean that you will leave us? Probably will come back to us when you find you are starving.

(*All sit except* PRECIOUS STREAM *and* HSIEH *whose chairs have been removed.*)

PRECIOUS S. That's far from the case. If I come back

to see you, dear mother, it will be when we can raise our heads higher than any of you can.

WANG. Poverty and failure will be your lot. But don't come to me for any help.

MADAM. Don't mind what your father says, dear. We shall always be ready to help you. But you're not really going to leave us for good, are you?

GOLDEN S. Please, don't, dear sister.

PRECIOUS S. (*crosses to R. below* HSIEH). I am afraid I'll have to. My place is to be by my husband's side for better or for worse.

(PROPERTY MAN L. *comes forward with two cushions and puts one in front of* WANG *as* PRECIOUS STREAM *crosses to kneel.*)

My dear father, your humble daughter, Precious Stream, pays her respects . . .

WANG (*rising and snatching away cushion*). No! You needn't consider me as your father.

(PROPERTY MAN *L. places second cushion.*)

PRECIOUS S. (*kneeling*). Then I must at least thank you for your share in my birth.

WANG. It was a mere accident.

(*Sees* MADAM—*sits quickly.* PRECIOUS STREAM *rises and crosses to below* HSIEH *at R.*)

SILVER S. And a sad one, too.

WANG. But I'll bet you'll be glad to leave him very soon.

PRECIOUS S. Do you dare to lay a wager definitely by clapping hands three times with me, father?

WANG. Certainly, and do you dare?

PRECIOUS S. Certainly.

ALL. Oh, please don't!

PRECIOUS S. (*to audience at C.*). I call upon all of you here to witness. To-day I hereby make a wager by clapping hands with my father three times, that my husband

and I will never come back to the Prime Minister's house unless we are rich and successful.

(PRECIOUS STREAM *goes upstage to below and R. of* WANG. WANG *rises and they clap hands three times.* WANG *sits—* PRECIOUS STREAM *returns to below* HSIEH.)

ALL. It can't be helped now.

PRECIOUS S. (*to* HSIEH). Now let us leave here for good and prepare for the wedding.

(*They go down C.*)

HSIEH (*to audience*). I will always honour you.

PRECIOUS S. (*to audience*). And I will obey you.

HSIEH (*turns R. to* PRECIOUS STREAM). I will protect you.

PRECIOUS S. (*turns L. to* HSIEH). I will love you.

(HSIEH *turns left and exits —* PRECIOUS STREAM *following.*)

WANG (*rising and going downstage—* MADAM *follows*). Disgraceful!

WEI. Disgusting!

SILVER S. Scandalous!

WANG. Let us retire!

(MUSIC *starts. They all move downstage.* WANG *bows to audience and exits L.,* MADAM *follows him after curtsying.* SU *and* GOLDEN STREAM *repeat the business. Then* WEI *and* SILVER STREAM *follow.* ATTENDANTS *and* MAIDS *come last but they do not bow or curtsy.* PROPERTY MEN *replace chairs to Left and Right and retire to off L. and off R.* MUSIC *stops.* LIGHTS *dim.*)

END OF ACT I

(*No Curtain.*)

(NOTE: There is no pause between Act I and Act II. As soon as the lights have faded on Act I the READER enters immediately.)

ACT II

(GONG NO. 1. *Enter* READER *from* D.L. SPOT *on* READER.)

HONOURABLE READER. By some accident we missed the simple but romantic marriage ceremony. Perhaps we purposely avoided it because we thought it might not turn out successfully, so it would be better to have nothing to do with the matter. Nevertheless we are always desirous to hear what happened to Precious Stream and Hsieh Ping-Kuei, and so we have kept in touch with them somehow or other. We decided that we may condescend to pay them a visit. Now that their honeymoon is over we will certainly not be considered as intruders. (Even if they object to our calling, we will go and watch them afar.) We arrive at the outside of the city at an open space before a kind of cave where the newly-married couple live. The open space in front of the cave and the interior of the cave are supposed to be represented here. And further, when circumstances render it necessary, the winding road on the little hill which leads to the cave is included in the scene. There is no decoration whatever on the stage and the audience must have recourse to their imagination.

(*Exit* READER L. GONG NO. 2—LIGHTS *up*. PROPERTY MEN *enter from* R. *and* L., *bow, etc.* GONG NO. 3—MUSIC *starts. Enter* 1ST *and* 2ND SOLDIERS. TWO SOLDIERS *enter* R. *downstage to* R.C. *and* L.C., *face each other, picking up bag of rice and firewood from* PROPERTY MAN R. *as they enter.* MUSIC *stops.*)

1ST SOLDIER. Here we are.

2ND SOLDIER. Yes, I believe this is the place.

1ST SOLDIER. Let us knock at the door.

(*He pretends to knock.* PROPERTY MAN L. *knocks on his box.*)

Is there any one there?

(Backs to audience.)

PRECIOUS S. *(offstage R.).*   Yes, I am coming.

(Enters R. down to C. addresses audience.)

If you are rich, even the most distant relations come to visit you; if you are poor not even the closest will come near you.   Since I married Hsieh Ping-Kuei we rarely have visitors.   But just now I heard a strange knocking at the door.

(Calls out.)

Who is knocking at the door?

1ST SOLDIER.   We have brought some firewood and rice for our eldest brother Hsieh.

(PRECIOUS STREAM goes round R. making a circle, as though descending steps, and comes to C. between them.)

PRECIOUS S.   Much obliged.

(Runs to door of cave.)

Please bring in what you have brought.

(They enter, and stand before her.)

1ST SOLDIER.   Here are ten hundredweight of firewood.

PRECIOUS S.   Put it here, please.

(PROPERTY MAN L. removes firewood.   PROPERTY MAN R. removes rice.)

2ND SOLDIER.   Here are five hundredweight of rice.

PRECIOUS S.   Put it here, please.   As your eldest brother, Hsieh, is not at home, you will excuse me for not asking you to stay and drink a cup of tea?

1ST SOLDIER.   Don't stand on ceremony.

2ND SOLDIER.   Thank you all the same.

PRECIOUS S.   Thank you for your trouble.   I won't detain you.

1ST SOLDIER.   Don't mention it.   Good-bye.

2ND SOLDIER.   Only too delighted.   Good-bye.

PRECIOUS S. (*curtsies*). Good-bye.

(PROPERTY MAN L. *places chair C.* PROPERTY MAN R. *does horses' hoofs for* HSIEH'S *entrance.* SOLDIERS *exit up L.* PRECIOUS STREAM *to C. sits and sews.*)

HSIEH (*offstage R.*). Look out! A horse is coming!

(*Enters R., picks up whip from* PROPERTY MAN'S *box R. Gallops down R. to C.*)

To a newly-married man an hour away from his home seems to be three years. So I feel I have been absent from my home for ages. As I have some important news for my dear wife, I must hurry on by whipping my horse.

(*He goes up L. round stage again, coming to C.*)

Here is my humble cave which I consider better than a splendid palace.

(*He ties horse R., giving whip to* PROPERTY MAN R. *He calls out and knocks as though to some one in a cave.*)

My dear third sister, will you kindly open the door?

PRECIOUS S. (*rises, goes up R. and round, comes out of cave*). Is that you, my lord and master, Hsieh, who has come back?

HSIEH. Yes, I have come back with some important news.

(PRECIOUS STREAM *opens door—they enter cave.*)

PRECIOUS S. Never mind about the news.

(HSIEH *enters, they both ascend stairs.*)

The most important thing is, do you want something to eat and drink?

(HSIEH *sits centre, she L. of him on stool placed by* PROPERTY MAN L.)

HSIEH. Thank you, I had a good dinner at the camp.

PRECIOUS S. So that's why the two soldiers brought us ten hundredweight of firewood and five hundredweight of rice.

HSIEH. Yes, that is part of the good news, too. It is payment in advance of my salary, and we needn't worry about our food any more.

PRECIOUS S. Good news, indeed!

HSIEH. I have just been appointed an officer of considerable rank.

PRECIOUS S. That's fairly good.

HSIEH. You don't seem to be very enthusiastic about the good news.

PRECIOUS S. Oh, yes, I am rather glad that you are now beginning to ascend the ladder of promotion. But this is only a beginning. To me, my husband ought not to be satisfied until he has at least conquered the world!

(He taps his forehead.)

And what else do you want to tell me? I perceive you've something on your mind that makes you uneasy.

HSIEH. Well, as I am now in government service, I can hardly consider myself as my own master. I am ordered abroad with the troops.

PRECIOUS S. A man's ambition cannot be limited by space, as the old proverb says. You needn't be uneasy about telling me you must leave for a time, though we have been married for a month only.

HSIEH *(still uneasy)*. Oh, quite—quite! But the fact is —is—well, it is a very long journey. We are going on a campaign to the Western Regions.

PRECIOUS S. *(astounded)*. Oh! It is a long and dangerous journey even in peaceful times; and now we are at war with them.

HSIEH. That's why I am going.

PRECIOUS S. Even those who go to the Western Regions as friends seldom return . . . I mean, seldom return satisfied.

HSIEH. No! They never return at all!

PRECIOUS S. And are you going there as their enemy!

HSIEH.   Yes, our aim is to conquer them.

PRECIOUS S.   When do you start?

HSIEH.   Very soon.

PRECIOUS S.   (*rising and crossing L.*).   Then I must prepare
some winter clothes for you, because you may have
to stay there over the new year.

HSIEH.   You needn't make any preparations for me.
I have something more to tell you.

PRECIOUS S.   Then tell me at once!

(Sits.)

HSIEH.   It is very difficult to tell you at once.

PRECIOUS S.   (*forcing a smile*).   Then tell me little by little.
I won't mind.

HSIEH (*sits*).   The date of our general mobilization is fixed.

PRECIOUS S.   (*anxiously*).   When?

HSIEH.   Well, do you understand riddles?

PRECIOUS S.   A little.

HSIEH (*hand business*).   If I say the date is far, far away——

PRECIOUS S.   (*forcing another smile*).   A hundred years away!

HSIEH.   And I say the date is quite, quite near at
hand——

PRECIOUS S.   (*appalled*).   To-day!   My heaven!

(She hides her face in her long sleeves.)

HSIEH (*rises, to R., turns and faces her*).   There!   There!
Cheer up!   Wouldn't you be glad to see me return
triumphantly on horseback as a General!   There is
something to which you may look forward!

PRECIOUS S.   But to think we have only been married
for a month, and you are leaving me to-day!   So un-
expectedly too!   Why did you apply for such a post?

HSIEH.   I didn't apply for it—it was conferred upon me.

PRECIOUS S.   How?

HSIEH (*resuming his seat C.*).   You know people have been

talking about a monster with a red mane which has
been devouring travellers in a wood nearby. Well, I
thought I ought to do something, and I went to the
wood this morning and shot the monster, which proved
to be merely a tiger of enormous size.

PRECIOUS S. (*looks at him*). A tiger of enormous size! And
you say 'merely.'

HSIEH. Yes. I was quite disappointed.

PRECIOUS S. Now, my dear hero, tell me how you did it!

HSIEH. Eh—oh—there is very little to tell. It was such
a trifle. I went there, I saw a tiger, I shot it, that's all!

PRECIOUS S. How fine! How grand!

HSIEH. Nonsense! Shooting an ordinary tiger when
anticipating a monster is as disappointing as shooting
a bird when hunting a tiger! One naturally feels a
come-down. And the worst of it is that people go
crazy and make a tremendous fuss about it.

PRECIOUS S. And make trouble, too!

HSIEH. Yes, terrible trouble! They actually carried me
to the Governor's yamen, where I was appointed a
captain and ordered to join the Western Punitive
Expedition. I found that Generals Wei and Su, our
brothers-in-law, are the joint commanders-in-chief of
this expedition, and I was ordered to mobilize with
the first company immediately!

(*Rises.*)

PRECIOUS S. Immediately!

(*Rises.*)

HSIEH (*gets cloth from* PROPERTY MAN R.). Yes, I was with
difficulty allowed to come back to bid you a hurried
good-bye, and I am afraid I have already overstayed
my time.

(*Rolls cloth on floor and pantomimes packing.*)

PRECIOUS S. Oh, no! You mustn't leave me like this!

HSIEH. I am afraid I must.

(PROPERTY MAN L. *removes chair and stool.* HSIEH *looks up at her.*)

Don't worry about me, the commanders-in-chief are our brothers-in-law, you see.

PRECIOUS S. I am more worried than ever on hearing that the wretch Wei is your chief. I don't trust him at all, and I hope you will take greatest care of yourself.

HSIEH. You needn't worry at all, for he is not going,

(*He gives cloth to* PRECIOUS STREAM, *who ties it on his back.*)

but staying behind to control the supply of ammunition and the paying of the soldiers. I have arranged that my pay is to be paid to you regularly in the form of rice and firewood, and he promised he would see to that. General Su will follow me with the main body of troops in a short time.

(*He goes out of cave, remains R.*)

PRECIOUS S. (*follows him, to L. of him*). That is excellent. I know how to deal with the wretch Wei, and I am relieved to hear that our brother-in-law Su is going to follow you soon.

A VOICE (*offstage L.*). Dear eldest brother, Hsieh, the troops are waiting for you!

HSIEH (*calling out*). Thank you! I will come at once.

(*To* PRECIOUS STREAM.)

I must go now. My dear third sister allow me to salute you and bid you good-bye.

(*He bows to her—she curtsies. He gets whip from* PROPERTY MAN R.)

PRECIOUS S. I must see my hero mount his steed.

HSIEH (*he mounts his horse*). My dear third sister, good-bye.

(*He starts going round stage, she following. Two complete circles are made.*)

PRECIOUS S. Farewell! I must see you riding along the winding road to the highway.

HSIEH. You will take care of yourself for my sake, won't you?

PRECIOUS S. (*following him carefully*). Of course! And you will take care of yourself for my sake, won't you?

HSIEH. Of course! Now please go back, my dear third sister.

PRECIOUS S. No, not until we reach the highway.

HSIEH (*stopping D.L.C., at end of 2nd circle*). Here is the highway. Go back and have a good rest.

PRECIOUS S. Do let me follow you for another short distance.

HSIEH. No, no! Although I can't bear to leave you, we must part sooner or later. The road is rough, and you are already tired. Please go back and rest.

PRECIOUS S. No, no! I must see you off from the camp.

HSIEH. Impossible! That's too far for you.

PRECIOUS S. I must. I must.

VOICE (*offstage L.*). We are starting, dear eldest brother, Hsieh.

HSIEH (*calling out*). I come, I come!

(*Pointing off R.*)

Look! There is your sister, Golden Stream, coming.

(PRECIOUS STREAM *looks off R.* HSIEH *draws his sword and cuts the reins, the cord on the whip, then gallops off.*)

PRECIOUS S. Oh! He has gone!

(*Exists L.* MUSIC *starts as* PRECIOUS STREAM *exits.* MUSIC *stops.* LIGHTS *fade. Immediately following,* MUSIC *starts.* LIGHTS *up.* MADAM *enters walking between the shafts of the carriage with* TWO ATTENDANTS *preceding her, followed by* DRIVER *and* TWO MAIDS. *They come downstage*—ATTENDANTS *to L.,* MADAM, *C.* MUSIC *stops.*)

MADAM. Since the news of the death of my son-in-law, Hsieh Ping-Kuei, reached me, I have been greatly worried about my dear daughter Precious Stream. She is very obstinate, and her pride won't allow her to accept any help from her father. It is now eight months since she left our house. As the New Year is drawing near and she is very poor, I have brought something with me, and have come to pay her a visit which I ought to have done a long time ago. We must be near the place now. It's not far from here, is it, driver?

DRIVER. No, Madam.

MADAM. Faster, please.

DRIVER. Yes, Madam.

(*They go round the stage once and arrive,* MADAM *standing R.C.,* DRIVER *and* MAIDS *behind her to R.,* ATTENDANTS *L.C.*)

1ST ATTENDANT. This is the cave, madam.

MADAM. Knock at the door, please.

1ST ATTENDANT (*knocking*). Lady Precious Stream, please open the door.

PRECIOUS S. (*enters L., crosses to C.*). I'm coming.

1ST ATTENDANT. Madam, your mother has come to visit you.

(ATTENDANTS *go L.*)

PRECIOUS S. (*C.*) Ah, this will kill me! Oh, how can I face my mother!

(*Comes out of cave.* MADAM *gets out of carriage.*)

Oh, my dear, dear mother.

MADAM (*puts arms round her*). My Precious Stream!

PRECIOUS S. How I have longed to see you, mother.

MADAM. And I to see you, but what a change! You, such a sweet-looking innocent little lamb now become a hollow-faced, starved looking ordinary person. Oh! I cannot bear this!

PRECIOUS S. Dear mother! Allow me to kneel down and pay my respects to you.

MADAM (*stopping her*). No, you mustn't stand on ceremony.

Attendants, draw near and pay your respects to Lady Precious Stream.

ALL. Our respects to you, Lady Precious Stream.

(SERVANTS *kneel and make curtsies.*)

PRECIOUS S. (*curtsies*). Many thanks. Please don't stand on ceremony.

MADAM. Now you may all go and have a rest, but return again in a short time.

ALL. Thank you, madam.

(*They exeunt L.*)

PRECIOUS S. Oh, dear mother, why do you condescend to come to our humble cave?

MADAM. I have heard that you are hungry and cold, and you are not well. So I wanted to see you and the place where you are living.

PRECIOUS S. (*barring the way*). Oh, no! My humble cave would profane your dignity.

MADAM. Nonsense! I must go in and see what kind of a life you are leading.

PRECIOUS S. It is a poor, wretched hole, and would only make you feel uncomfortable.

MADAM (*firmly*). The place where my dear daughter can live for nearly a year is at least good enough for me to visit!

PRECIOUS S. (*giving in*). Then let me go in first and have the place tidied for you.

MADAM. No, I want to see it just as it is. Lead the way, my darling.

(*They enter cave,* PRECIOUS STREAM *leading the way, taking* MADAM'S *hand. They go round stage finish with* PRECIOUS STREAM *L.C.,* MADAM *C.*)

PRECIOUS S. Mind the steps, mother dear.

MADAM. So this is your place!

(PROPERTY MAN R. *places chair C.* PROPERTY MAN L. *brings stool places it, L. of* MADAM.)

Oh, you silly darling, fancy your forsaking your beautifully decorated boudoir and coming to this horrible cave! How could you!

PRECIOUS S. (*offering her a chair*). Make yourself comfortable in this poor chair, dear mother.

(PROPERTY MAN L. *brings bowl and chop-sticks above* PRECIOUS STREAM. *She takes them from him, and gives them to* MADAM, *who gives them to* PROPERTY MAN R.)

I am afraid I have no tea or refreshments to offer you, except some poor rice.

MADAM. Fancy sacrificing the delicacies you enjoyed for this poor stuff! How could you? Now, sit down yourself.

PRECIOUS S. (*sitting on the left side*). Thank you, dear mother! After those delicacies this plain fare seemed to be very palatable to me.

MADAM. You are under-nourished. That's why you are ill.

PRECIOUS S. Indeed it is not a question of food. The wretched Wei told me that my husband had been killed! It was this news that sent me to bed.

MADAM. This news may be false, my darling.

PRECIOUS S. Oh, yes! I don't believe it at all. But, still, it makes me feel wretched. And father sends agents to try to persuade me to marry again, which makes me feel worse.

MADAM (*furious*). The old rascal! He'll wish he'd never been born when I've done talking to him to-night.

PRECIOUS S. Oh, no! Please don't quarrel with father on *my* account. It will only increase my sin against filial piety.

MADAM. Very well, then. He has you to thank if I let him off. How are you feeling now?

PRECIOUS S. You see I have already recovered at the sight of you!

MADAM. But this is not the place for convalescence. Now be reasonable, and come back with your mother, where you need not worry about anything, and will have plenty to eat and plenty to wear.

PRECIOUS S. No, dear mother . . . I'd rather starve here than go back.

MADAM. Nonsense! Now tell me, when did you last hear from your husband?

PRECIOUS S. I have never heard from him since his departure. The official news declared that there was a general defeat. Not long ago when the troops of the Western Region retired, our search party returned with the report that my husband was amongst those who were killed.

MADAM. Oh, my dear, let us hope that he has escaped somehow and will return safe and sound!

PRECIOUS S. Thank you, dear mother! But I had hoped he would return victorious. To return as a deserter or an escaped prisoner, would be worse than not to return at all.

MADAM. Oh, brave girl. I think the best way for you is to come back with me, and if your father tries to say anything against you he will have *me* to deal with.

PRECIOUS S. (*determined*). No! I am afraid you'll have to go back alone, dear mother. And if father refers to me, tell him to regard me as dead or still better, regard me as never having been born.

MADAM. Don't be stupid. Don't mind your father. Don't worry about your husband! Come to your mother! The place where your mother is, is the place for you; and the place where your mother goes is the place where you should go. Your mother will protect you. And when your mother dies you will be her chief mourner, won't you?

PRECIOUS S. Of course, of course!

MADAM. And when your father dies don't mourn for him, and don't weep for him at all.

PRECIOUS S. (*coaxing her*). No, no, I won't weep for him at all. It is you, and only you, whom I love and whom I will mourn and weep for. Do you feel satisfied now?

MADAM. Yes. But since you refuse to go with me, I will stay with you here instead.

PRECIOUS S. (*rises*). Oh, no! You can't stay here.

MADAM. I am determined.

PRECIOUS S. (*crosses D.L.*). This will never do!

(*The* SERVANTS, MAIDS *and* DRIVER *return from R. and stop D.R.*)

MADAM. You can't force me to go.

PRECIOUS S. I hear the servants coming. I think you ought to go now, dear mother.

(PROPERTY MAN L. *moves stool.*)

MADAM (*rises*). No. My maids, bring in the silver and the rice and the clothes that you have brought with you.

MAIDS. Yes, madam.

(*They enter and ascend stairs.*)

MADAM. Give them to Lady Precious Stream.

MAIDS. Yes, madam.

(*They cross to L. of* PRECIOUS STREAM.)

MAIDS. These are for you, Lady Precious Stream.

MADAM. Put them down.

PRECIOUS S. No, mother. I won't take anything from the Wang family.

(MAIDS *put down parcels. They are removed by* PROPERTY MAN L. MAIDS *return to positions D.R.*)

MADAM. Nonsense! These are presents from me to you.

They have nothing to do with the Wang family. Besides, when I am staying with you, we shall need a little money to buy some extra food. You can't expect me to live on rice pudding all the time.

PRECIOUS S. Dear mother, you can't stay here with me.

MADAM. Can't I? You'll see. Attendants!

ATTENDANTS (*kneeling*). Yes, madam?

MADAM. All of you may go home now, for I'm going to stay a few days here with Lady Precious Stream.

(*She sits.*)

ATTENDANTS (*rising*). Yes, madam.

PRECIOUS S. Wait, please. What shall I do? What shall I do? (*Tapping her forehead.*) Ah! I have it. Well, mother, I have changed my mind. I agree to return with you rather than let you stay here with me.

MADAM (*rising*). That's a good girl. Attendants! Prepare the carriage for us. Lead the way, my darling.

(*They commence to go out of cave.* ATTENDANTS *cross to* D.L. DRIVER *arranges carriage.* PROPERTY MAN R. *removes chair.*)

PRECIOUS S. Mind the steps, mother. Oh, mother, I forgot something.

MADAM. What is it, my darling?

PRECIOUS S. I forgot to put the silver, the clothes and the rice in a safe place.

MADAM. They won't be lost if the cave door is locked.

PRECIOUS S. But the rats—they will eat the rice and destroy the clothes.

(*Both enter carriage.*)

MADAM. They are worth very little. I can afford to get some more.

PRECIOUS S. I can't allow anything from my dear mother to be destroyed. I won't be a moment.

MADAM. Then be quick.

(PROPERTY MAN L. *places cushion after* PRECIOUS STREAM *has gone into cave;* PRECIOUS STREAM *runs into the cave, bolts door and falls on her knees C.*)

PRECIOUS S.   Mother, I am not going back with you. And for my unfilial conduct I am kneeling inside the cave.

MADAM.   Oh, my obstinate darling, how could you?

PRECIOUS S.   Dear mother, though I remain in the cave, my heart goes with you.

MADAM (*to the* MAIDS).   My maids, try to get Lady Precious Stream to open the door and come with me.

(MAIDS *cross L. to R. of* PRECIOUS STREAM. PROPERTY MAN L. *knocks on his box as* MAIDS *pretend to knock on cave door.*)

1ST MAID (*knocks at cave*).   Lady Precious Stream, will you please open the door and come back with us?

PRECIOUS S.   No, dear maids. I sincerely entreat you instead of trying to persuade me to come out, to try your best to make Madam, my mother, depart as quickly as possible. The weather is cold and the north wind is bitter. If you will do this favour for me, you will have the eternal gratitude of an unfilial daughter.

MAIDS.   We will, we will!

(*They move R. to above* MADAM.)

1ST MAID.   Madam, Lady Precious Stream refuses to come out. She entreats you to return as soon as possible for it is bitterly cold here.

2ND MAID.   If you will allow me to say a word, Madam. I think she is quite determined, and we had better go home ourselves and come back some other time.

MADAM (*weeping*).   Oh, my poor darling daughter.

PRECIOUS S. (*weeping*).   Oh, my poor dear mother.

1ST MAID (*to the servants*).   I think we had better start at once.

(MAIDS *return to places behind* DRIVER.)

MADAM. Start!

(*They go round stage once and exit L.* PRECIOUS STREAM
listens to them leave and comes out of cave to C. PROPERTY
MAN L. *takes away the cushion from* PRECIOUS STREAM.)

PRECIOUS S. Oh, she has gone!

(MUSIC *starts. As* PRECIOUS STREAM *exits:* MUSIC *stops.*
STAGE LIGHTS *fade.* HOUSE LIGHTS *on.*)

END OF ACT II

(*No Curtain*)

(During the intermission the PROPERTY MEN re-arrange
their prop. boxes, sweep stage, etc.)

ACT III

HONOURABLE READER. We are now coming to a strange land known as the Western Regions. It is believed that the customs here are exactly opposite those of China. For instance, the women wear long gowns whilst the men wear short coats and have their trousers showing. Their appearance, too, is unusual. They have red hair, green eyes, prominent noses and hairy hands.

The stage represents the magnificent court of the King of the Western Regions. Probably they have very queer furniture and very strange decorations. Indeed we would be quite at a loss to prepare the properties of this scene had we not the advantage of leaving the audience to furnish them according to their imagination.

Everything in this scene is strange. But the most strange thing of all is that HIS MAJESTY THE KING is no other than our old friend the gardener, HSIEH PING-KUEI! He whom we believed the enemy killed long ago, is still alive, and after his conquest of the Western Regions has proclaimed himself King. To our regret no records of this conquest exist and we regret even more having arrived just a day too late to see his coronation.

However, another great occasion is coming very soon. It has been arranged that a royal wedding is to take place to-morrow. The Queen Elect is a foreign Princess with whom our hero shares the laurels of his victories. She is another clever woman who has succeeded in making our hero put a halter willingly around his own neck. There is a general rumour to the effect that there is a reluctance on his part to the marriage, and the people wonder why such a beautiful maiden should not be snapped up with alacrity. But

we know that the cause is not due to this excellent
lady whom we are going to meet soon, but to HIS
MAJESTY, who has some dark secret that he dares not
reveal. That is why we find that the first gentleman
of the kingdom is rather depressed in this hour of
what should be great happiness.

He seems to know that among the audience many are
doubtful of his identity so he introduces himself to
them once more.

(READER *exits R.*)

(GONG NO. 2. STAGE LIGHTS *up*. PROPERTY MEN *enter
L. and R.* GONG NO. 3—MUSIC *starts. Enter* 1ST *and* 2ND
ATTENDANTS *followed by* HSIEH. ATTENDANTS *cross to
D.R. and D.L.* HSIEH *to D.C.* MUSIC *stops.*)

HSIEH (*saluting*). By the help of the Royal Princess I have
now the honour to be your humble servant Hsieh
Ping-Kuei, the King of the Western Regions. I have
been away from my home for eighteen years. There
are two things I desire perpetually: to return to my
wife, Precious Stream, and to avenge myself on Wei,
the Tiger General, who attempted to have me murdered and nearly caused my death. When I returned
victorious, General Wei pretended to celebrate my
triumph by giving a banquet in his camp, and having
made me quite intoxicated with strong wine, tied me
on to a horse and set it galloping towards the enemy.

(PROPERTY MAN L. *places table C.* PROPERTY MAN R.
places chair C. above table.)

Luckily I was rescued by the Princess, who released me
and helped me conquer all the Western Regions, from
which she revolted for love of me. She wishes to marry
me, an unusual proposal which I could not possibly
refuse. Postponing it again and again I have at last
been obliged to promise to marry her after my
coronation.

(*Crosses U.C. sits.*)

Whilst every one else in the kingdom seems to be

rejoicing at the prospect of the coming wedding, I alone am troubled by it.

(PROPERTY MAN R. *places chair D.R. for* WILD GOOSE. WILD GOOSE *enters from R. crosses D.R. on to chair.*)

I have been vainly trying to explain to her that I am already married, but I can't bear to break her heart. What shall I do? What *shall* I do?

WILD GOOSE.   Hsieh Ping-Kuei's unfaithful!

(*The* WILD GOOSE *continues to repeat this phrase over and over, sotto voce, until shot.*)

ATTENDANTS.   We beg to report to your Majesty that a wild goose is flying over the palace, uttering strange sounds.

HSIEH (*rises, crosses D.L.C.*).   Show me where it is.

ATTENDANTS (*pointing*).   There is the bird, Your Majesty.

HSIEH.   This is strange.   It seems to keep uttering that I'm unfaithful.   This is, indeed, a bad omen.   Attendants, bring me my bow and arrows.

ATTENDANTS.   Yes, Your Majesty.

(1ST ATTENDANT *gets bow from* PROPERTY MAN L. *and gives it to* HSIEH.)

HSIEH.   I have never before heard a wild goose uttering sounds which seem to be like the words of a human being.   With my bow and arrow I shoot it!   There!

(*He shoots.* WILD GOOSE *makes movements as though shot and exits R.* 2ND ATTENDANT *gets piece of cloth from* PROPERTY MAN R.)

2ND ATTENDANT.   I beg to report to Your Majesty that I found this piece of cloth on the bird.

HSIEH (*crossing to C.*).   Give it to me.

2ND ATTENDANT (*handing it to him*).   Yes, Your Majesty.

HSIEH (*after looking at cloth*).   Ah!   Attendants, retire for a moment, please.

(ATTENDANTS *exit L. and R.*)

The words on the cloth, torn from her skirt, are written with her blood. They say: 'Precious Stream presents her respects to her unfaithful husband Hsieh Ping-Kuei and begs to tell him that since his departure she has been suffering every hardship in the humble cave. If he returns immediately, they may meet each other once more, but if he delays for only a few days, they may never see each other again.' Oh, my dear wife, my dear Precious Stream. I cannot stop the tears flowing from my eyes. Far, far away there is my home, my sweet home. My dear wife. I must get back in time to see you. Let me ponder and think of some plan. Ah! I have it!

(ATTENDANTS *enter from R. and L. to D.R. and D.L.*)

I must do it. I must do it at any cost. Attendants!

ATTENDANTS. Yes, Your Majesty.

HSIEH. Request Her Highness, the Royal Princess, to come to court.

(*He sits U.R.*)

ATTENDANTS. Yes, Your Majesty.

(*Crosses U.R. and U.L. and call off R.*)

His Majesty requests the presence of Her Highness, the Royal Princess.

PRINCESS (*off R.*). To hear is to obey.

(MUSIC *starts. Enter* FOUR MAIDS *from R.* 1ST *and* 2ND *cross D.R. and then go to D.L.* 3RD *and* 4TH *cross D.R.* PRINCESS *follows to D.C.* ATTENDANTS *return to places D.L. and D.R.* MUSIC *stops.*)

PRINCESS (*to audience, saluting*). Your humble maid, the Royal Princess of the Western Regions, at your service. I have just returned from the parade grounds after reviewing my troops and have been told that His Majesty has commanded me to go to court.

(*To* MAIDS.)

My maids, lead the way to the court.

MAIDS (*saluting*).   Yes, Your Highness.

(*The* MAIDS *cross to C. and then go U.L., and make a large circle around the stage, returning to their original positions. The* PRINCESS *follows them but stops at R. of table.*)

PRINCESS (*to* HSIEH, *saluting*).   Your humble maid, the Royal Princess of the Western Regions, offers her respects to Your Majesty.

HSIEH.   Don't stand on ceremony.

(PROPERTY MAN L. *places chair at L. of table.*)

PRINCESS (*crossing below table to chair L.*).   Thank you.

HSIEH.   You are at liberty to sit down.

(MAIDS *cross directly to U.L.C. and U.R.C., standing above chairs.*)

PRINCESS (*sitting*).   Thank you.   May I know what important affair of State Your Majesty wishes to discuss with me?

HSIEH.   There is no affair of State I wish to trouble you with.   As you have been having a very hard time recently in reviewing all these troops, I have prepared a banquet in your honour, and I would be glad if you would consent to have a hearty carousal with me.

PRINCESS (*highly pleased*).   This would indeed be a great honour!   Allow me to serve Your Majesty with wine.

HSIEH (*signals* ATTENDANT *R.*).   Oh, no, I couldn't possibly trouble you.   Attendants!   Prepare wine for me.

ATTENDANTS.   Yes, Your Majesty.

HSIEH (*to* PRINCESS).   Let me have the pleasure of serving you.

(1ST ATTENDANT *gets tray with wine jug and two glasses from* PROPERTY MAN R. *puts them on table, then back to his place.* HSIEH *immediately pours out wine, hands glass to* PRINCESS. *She drinks.*)

Although I am very happy in drinking with you, the thought of our being attacked by the neighbouring States constantly troubles me.

PRINCESS. I beg your Majesty not to worry about the invasion of other States, for I myself am able to cope with any invasion of the enemy, regardless of the numbers.

HSIEH. Regardless of number.

PRINCESS. Yes! But of course we entirely depend upon your blessing, without which there is no chance of victory.

HSIEH. Oh, no, you are the invincible Princess.

PRINCESS. Thank you. To Your Majesty's health!

> (*She finds that her cup is empty.*)

More wine to Your Majesty!

HSIEH. How full of life and charm you are!

> (*Pours more wine.*)

Do not hesitate to refresh yourself thoroughly. You have had a hard time reviewing the troops, and a good bumper of wine will greatly benefit you.

PRINCESS (*pleased*). Oh, thanks, Your Majesty! But I can't drink as much as I could formerly.

HSIEH. How much could you drink formerly?

PRINCESS. A hundred cups at least!

HSIEH. And now?

PRINCESS (*smiling*). Only fifty cups (*strikes two cups together*), multiplied by two.

HSIEH (*laughing*). Ha, ha! Just the same! One hundred cups!

> (*To* ATTENDANTS.)

Attendants! Serve the wine in large cups!

ATTENDANTS. Yes, Your Majesty.

> (MUSIC *starts.* ATTENDANT L. *removes tray and glasses from table, giving them to* PROPERTY MAN L. ATTENDANT R. *gets tray and two goblets and jug from* PROPERTY MAN R., *places them on table, then back to their places.* HSIEH *pours out and gives* PRINCESS *goblet of wine. She drinks it, hands*

it to MAID *who passes it along to the* MAID R. *who places it on table.* HSIEH *repeats business goblet passed round, replaced on table.* HSIEH *then gives the* PRINCESS *the jug, who sways in her seat and gradually sinks with head on table.* MUSIC *stops.*)

MAIDS (*look first at* PRINCESS, *then at each other, then speak to audience*). Her Highness is intoxicated.

HSIEH (*raising her head*). So she is. (*Rises.*) She has fallen into my trap.

(PROPERTY MAN L. *puts flag in* PRINCESS'S *belt.* HSIEH *moves to R. of* PRINCESS, *takes flag from her belt, then down to C. to audience.*)

Now I have done it. With this little flag I can go where I like, and get away from the Western Regions, but I shall have to leave without bidding her good-bye.

(PROPERTY MAN R. *puts pen and paper on table, removes goblets and jug.*)

HSIEH (*sits at table*). I will write a letter to her, I can't bear to say good-bye to her.

(*Reading as he writes.*)

'I am going to the frontier to review the troops there. If you still love me, follow me with all your troops to the third pass; if you don't love me, stay where you are and don't think of me.'

(*He rises.*)

Men of the Western Region, saddle my horse!

ATTENDANTS. Yes, Your Majesty.

(2ND ATTENDANT *gets whip from* PROPERTY MAN R. *holds it for* HSIEH, *who takes it.* HSIEH *leaps on his horse and gallops off L.* MAIDS *step forward, waving hands.*)

MAIDS. Your Highness! Your Highness!

(MAIDS *return to place upstage.*)

PRINCESS (*waking up*). The wine has affected me a little. Where is His Majesty?

(*Looks under table.*)

1ST ATTENDANT. His Majesty has gone to the frontier to review the troops there, Your Highness.

PRINCESS. Did he leave any orders for me?

2ND ATTENDANT (*picks up letter from table, hands it to her*). His Majesty left this letter for Your Highness.

(PRINCESS *takes letter.*)

PRINCESS (*rising*). Let me read it. What does he mean? What *does* he mean?

(*Pacing stage, tapping forehead.*)

Ah, I see! His Majesty has gone back to China. He wants me to follow him with all the troops to China. Attendants!

(*Turns back to audience.*)

ATTENDANTS. Yes, Your Highness.

PRINCESS. Order my two aides-de-camp Ma Ta and Kiang Hai to await my further orders before the palace gates with all my troops.

ATTENDANTS. Yes, Your Highness.

(PROPERTY MAN L. *clears chair* PRINCESS *has used.* PROPERTY MAN R. *moves arm-chair.* PROPERTY MAN L. *clears table to upstage L.* ATTENDANTS *cross U.L. and U.R., turn R. and call:*)

Her Highness orders her two aides-de-camp Ma Ta and Kiang Hai to await her further orders before the palace gates with all her troops.

MA TA and KIANG HAI (*offstage*). To hear is to obey.

(ATTENDANTS *return to places D.L. and D.R.*)

PRINCESS (*facing audience*). How unreasonable His Majesty is. He ought not to have gone away without bidding me good-bye. I will overtake him with my troops and ask him what is the reason.

(PRINCESS, *facing her maids, gestures them to precede her.* MAIDS *salute, face L., march off L., followed by* ATTENDANTS *and* PRINCESS. *Enter* MA TA *and* KIANG HAI *R. getting spears from* PROPERTY MAN *R., downstage to C., to audience.*)

MA TA. Our home is far, far in the North-West.

KIANG HAI. We are somewhat tongue-tied.

MA TA. Beef and mutton are what we like best!

KIANG HAI. Big camels are what we ride.

MA TA (*saluting*). I am Ma Ta, at your service.

KIANG HAI. I am Kiang Hai, your humble servant.

MA TA. Glad to see you.

KIANG HAI. How goes it?

MA TA and KIANG HAI. We are here waiting for orders from Her Highness, the Royal Princess.

(*They take one step back, turn, face each other, two steps back. Enter* MAIDS, *two down R., two L. followed by* PRINCESS *who comes C.* MAIDS *gets spears and* PRINCESS'S *whip from* PROPERTY MAN *R.*)

PRINCESS. Oh, unfaithful Hsieh Ping-Kuei, I will overtake you and sue you for breach of promise.

MA TA and KIANG HAI (*saluting*). Our respects to you, Your Highness.

PRINCESS. Don't stand on ceremony. Are the troops ready?

MA TA and KIANG HAI. Yes, Your Highness. We are waiting for your orders.

PRINCESS. Order them to march to the first pass.

MA TA and KIANG HAI (*calling*). To the first pass.

(MUSIC *starts.* MAIDS *L. turn upstage, start marching, followed by* MAIDS *R. They exit L. followed by* MA TA, KIANG HAI *and* PRINCESS. *Pass brought on R.* WARDEN *comes on R. stands on chair behind it. Pass brought on by* SOLDIERS 1 *and* 2. MUSIC *stops.*)

WARDEN. By the order of Her Highness the Royal Princess of the Western Regions, I am the Warden of the first pass.

(HSIEH *enters R., downstage to D.L.*)

HSIEH. Hey! Open the pass for me!

WARDEN. Where do you come from, and what is your business?

HSIEH. By the orders of Her Highness the Royal Princess, I have business of State to transact beyond the pass.

WARDEN. Have you the yellow flag from Her Highness.

HSIEH. Yes—here it is.

WARDEN. Soldiers, open the pass for him!

(MUSIC *starts.* HSIEH *upstage, through the pass and off L.* MAIDS *enter, march to L., make line up and down stage,* MA TA *and* KIANG HAI *following them. A division is left between the* FOUR MAIDS. PRINCESS *enters R. across to L., comes to L.C. through the division between* MAIDS. MUSIC *stops.*)

WARDEN. The Warden of the first pass pays his respects to you, Your Highness.

PRINCESS. Don't stand on ceremony. I want to ask you, has His Majesty the King passed here?

WARDEN (*trembling*). There was a man who passed through, but I don't know if it was His Majesty the King.

PRINCESS. Don't you even know your King? You are under arrest! To the second pass.

(MUSIC *starts.* MAID NO. I *starts, followed by other* MAIDS, MA TA *and* KIANG HAI. *They march in front of* PRINCESS. *She follows them. All go through pass and exit L. Pass is moved to C stage. Warden changes beard.* MUSIC *stops.*)

WARDEN. By order of her Royal Highness, the Princess of the Western Regions, I am the Warden of the second pass.

(HSIEH *enters R., down L.*)

HSIEH. Hey! Open the pass for me!

WARDEN. Where do you come from and what is your business?

HSIEH. By the order of Her Highness the Royal Princess, I have business of State to transact beyond the pass.

WARDEN.   Have you the yellow flag from Her Highness?

HSIEH.   Yes, here it is!

WARDEN.   Soldiers, open the pass for him.

(MUSIC *starts.* HSIEH *goes through the pass and off* L. MAIDS *march in as before below pass to* L. *leaving division between them for* PRINCESS. PRINCESS *enters* R. *through the division to* L.C. MUSIC *stops.*)

The Warden of the second pass presents his respects to Your Highness.

PRINCESS.   Don't stand on ceremony.   I want to ask you. Has His Majesty the King passed here?

WARDEN.   A man did pass here, but——

PRINCESS.   Excellent service you're rendering me.   Report yourself for a court martial to-morrow morning.   To the third pass!

(MUSIC *starts.* MAIDS, MA TA, KIANG HAI *and* PRINCESS *march through pass and exit* L. *as before.* WARDEN *joins in the march after* MAIDS *and before* MA TA *and exits with them. Pass is moved to* L. MU *enters and stands on chair behind pass.* MUSIC *stops.*)

MU.   I am well known for my white helmet, white armour, and white banners.   I also have a white moustache, white beard, and white eyebrows.   After I have drunk plenty of white wine I will show you the whites of my eyes!   I am old Mu, the White General, at your service.   By order of His Imperial Majesty, the Emperor, I am the Warden of the Third Pass.

(HSIEH *enters* R. *down to* C.)

HSIEH (*to audience*).   Wait!   This is now the frontier of my motherland.   The third pass is the boundary.   The man in the tower seems to be old General Mu.   Let me call him by name.

(*Crosses up to pass.*)

My respects to you, Old General Mu.

MU. Thank you. Thank you. Who are you to call me by name?

HSIEH. I am Captain Hsieh Ping-Kuei coming back from the Western Regions to report myself at head-quarters.

MU. The pass is haunted! The pass is haunted!

(MU *gets down behind the pass.* SOLDIERS *shake the pass.*)

You were killed in the Western Regions. So this is your spirit which comes back to haunt us.

HSIEH. No, I was not killed. My enemy planned my death and thinks I am dead but I am still alive.

MU (*poking head through pass*). Is that so? I can hardly believe it.

MAIDS (*off.*) Houp-hey!

HSIEH. There are troops in pursuit of me. Open the pass and let me in.

MU. All right. Open the pass for him, soldiers.

(MUSIC *starts.* HSIEH *goes through pass and exits. L.* MAIDS *enter from R. followed by* MA TA *and* KIANG HAI. *They form a line as before. The* PRINCESS *goes between them to C. All are very tired.* MUSIC *stops.*)

MA TA and KIANG HAI. We beg to report to Your Highness that we have now arrived at the third pass, which belongs to China.

PRINCESS (*crossing R.*). So we have! Go and ask them to let us pass through.

MA TA and KIANG HAI (*crossing L.*). Yes, Your Highness.

PRINCESS (*turning L.*). One moment. Come back!

MA TA and KIANG HAI (*turning R.*). Yes, Your Highness.

PRINCESS. As we have come to the territory of another country we must be more polite in our speech!

MA TA and KIANG HAI. Yes, Your Highness.

(*They face old Mu.*)

MA TA. Hey! My old man!

MU. Old moon? Can't see the old moon until midnight.

KIANG HAI. My master!

MU. Mustard! Go to the grocery for it.

MA TA. My Lord!

MU. He is in Heaven.

KIANG HAI. My Emperor!

MU. You are empty? This is not an eating-house. What are you two doing here? You are too ugly to be called human beings, and certainly too ordinary to be called devils. Go back, and get some one more presentable to talk to me.

(They turn to PRINCESS.*)*

MA TA *and* KIANG HAI. He requests the presence of Your Highness.

PRINCESS. All right. I'll go.

(She goes to upper corner of the pass. MA TA *and* KIANG HAI *return to their places in line.)*

My respects to you, old grandfather in the tower.

MU. Thank you, and mine to the little grandmother beneath it. What is your business here?

PRINCESS. May I ask you, has His Majesty the King of our country, Captain Hsieh Ping-Kuei of your country, passed through this way?

MU. His Majesty the King of your country has not passed, but Captain Hsieh Ping-Kuei of our country has passed.

PRINCESS. But he is no other than the King of our country. If he has passed here and is with you there, I entreat you to ask him to appear on the wall of the pass, so that we may say a few words to each other. Then I will withdraw with my forces, and I promise you there will be no trouble and no damage. Do you think this can be done, my old General?

MU. You bewitching little minx! Captain Hsieh Ping-Kuei of our country used to be a robust young giant, and now, after eighteen years adventure in your country, he comes back the wreck of a man! How can I allow him to see you again, you little minx!

PRINCESS (*furious*). What impudence! (*Crosses R.*) Ma Ta and Kiang Hai!

MA TA and KIANG HAI. Yes, Your Highness!

PRINCESS. Attack the Pass!

ALL. Houp-Hey!!

(*All take one step forward as if to attack pass with spears.*)

MU. Wait a moment! Wait a moment! The pass is made of cloth; it will be damaged if you don't take care.

(PRINCESS *motions them to stand at ease again.*)

If you withdraw for a short distance, I will ask Captain Hsieh Ping-Kuei, to come out and speak to you. After all, I am not his guardian, and I don't care what company he keeps!

PRINCESS (*crosses to pass*). You must play fair!

MU. Of course! Fair play for a fair lady.

PRINCESS. The troops are ordered to withdraw to a short distance.

(*They all do a left-turn.*)

MA TA and KIANG HAI. Yes, Your Highness.

(*They march off R., MAIDS going off first.*)

MU. Captain Hsieh! Captain Hsieh!

HSIEH (*appearing from the L.*) May I congratulate you on your victory?

MU. Congratulate the lady, my enemy! The victory belongs to her. You are requested to go up to the tower; she wants to speak to you.

(*Gets down from chair.*)

HSIEH. Thank you for your trouble.

(MU *exits L.*)

I see the Princess coming alone.

PRINCESS (*appearing again*). I see the unfaithful one standing alone.

(*To* HSIEH.)

What have I done to deserve this? Why did you desert me?

HSIEH. I will tell you everything now. The other day a wild goose brought a letter from Lady Precious Stream.

PRINCESS. What! Who is this Lady Precious Stream?

HSIEH. She is my wife!

PRINCESS (*appalled.*) What—your wife! So you are already married! You are going back to her now?

HSIEH. Yes.

PRINCESS. Oh, you have been deceiving me all these years!

HSIEH (*protesting*). No. You wrong me there! I was desperately in love with you all the time, and I am still.

PRINCESS. Then why do you forsake me?

HSIEH. Because I am in honour bound to the other.

PRINCESS. But you ought to have told me this before.

HSIEH. I loved you too much to hurt your feelings.

PRINCESS. To deceive me and then desert me is most heartless.

(*Crosses D.R.*)

I will never speak to you again. I hate you! I hate you!

HSIEH (*hurt*). Please don't! I *still* love you. Will you be a sister to me, and go to China with me?

PRINCESS. Never. Never! I don't want to be near you now.

HSIEH. But I want to be near you. That's why I asked you to follow me.

PRINCESS. Yes, but at a safe distance.

HSIEH. Don't say that. I would gladly marry you if I

could. Now, will you not be my sister and come with me?

PRINCESS. Never!

HSIEH. Then I must bid you farewell for ever, because I may never see you again!

PRINCESS. I don't want to see you again!

HSIEH. I have many enemies in China, and without your military protection I shall probably be murdered by them very soon!

PRINCESS. Oh, I never thought of that! Yes, your General Wei will try to murder you. I must go with you to protect you, even if I hate you.

(Crosses few steps L.)

HSIEH. No! I can't accept your protection if you still hate me.

PRINCESS *(crosses a step L.)* Well, I won't hate you.

HSIEH. And will be my sister?

PRINCESS *(crosses a step L.)*. No! At most your cousin.

HSIEH. No! Sister.

PRINCESS *(crosses a step L.)*. Let us say first cousin?

HSIEH. No! Sister.

PRINCESS *(crosses to C.)*. All right. Come down at once.

HSIEH. No! In Lady Precious Stream's letter she said she is in great danger, so I must hurry on. Order your troops to be encamped near the pass and await a message from me. Good-bye till then.

(HSIEH exits L., followed by SOLDIERS carrying pass.)

PRINCESS. Good-bye.

(Calling off R.)

Ma Ta and Kiang Hai!

MA TA and KIANG HAI *(off R.)*. Yes, Your Highness.

PRINCESS. Order the troops to be encamped here.

MA TA and KIANG HAI. Yes, Your Highness.

(MUSIC *starts*. MAIDS *enter from* R. *followed by* MA TA *and* KIANG HAI. *They cross stage and exit* L., *followed by the* PRINCESS. LIGHTS *dim*. MUSIC *stops*. LIGHTS *up*.)

HSIEH. Look out! A horse is coming!

(*Enters from* R. *Crosses to* D.C.)

When one is anxious to get home one travels both in day time and by starlight. Bidding good-bye to the Princess not long ago, I have now arrived at the little hill not far from my own door.

(*He dismounts to* R., *gives whip to* PROPERTY MAN R.)

Let me tie my horse under the shadow of a willow tree.

(*To audience.* PRECIOUS STREAM *enters from* L., *gets basket from* PROPERTY MAN L. *During the following speech she crosses* D.L., *then crosses stage to* D.R.)

There is some one coming. She looks rather like my wife, but I must be careful to avoid being guilty of taking another man's wife as my own. Now that I have arrived at my home, I must be very polite.

(*Crosses to* D.L., *faces* R. *and bows*.)

My respects to you, madam. May I have a word with you?

PRECIOUS S. (*faces* L., *curtsies*). And mine to you. Have you lost your way, sir?

HSIEH (*crossing to* D.L.C.). No one could be lost in such a place as this. I want to find some one.

PRECIOUS S. (*crossing to* D.R.C.). Only famous people are known to me.

HSIEH. She whom I seek is a very famous person. She is the daughter of the Prime Minister Wang, and the wife of Hsieh Ping-Kuei. Lady Precious Stream she is by name.

PRECIOUS S. May I ask why you are inquiring for her?

HSIEH. I have been serving in the same company as her husband, who has entrusted me with a letter for her.

PRECIOUS S. Let me have the letter.

HSIEH. Oh, no, madam. Hsieh Ping-Kuei said this letter should be delivered in person—by me.

PRECIOUS S. Please excuse me a moment.

HSIEH. Certainly.

> (*He crosses U.L. to* PROPERTY MAN *and gets tea.*)

PRECIOUS S. (*crosses to audience*). I should like to confess and get that letter at once, but I am in such rags that I am ashamed to do so, and if I don't he will certainly not give me that letter. Oh, how cruel that for eighteen long years' separation we have never met and have not been able to correspond. What shall I do?

> (*Business of tapping forehead.*)

Ah! I have it.

> (*Turns to* HSIEH, *who has come back D.L.C.*)

Well, sir, do you understand riddles?

HSIEH. A little.

PRECIOUS S. Do you want to see Precious Stream?

HSIEH. Yes.

PRECIOUS S. (*hand bus.*) Now, if you look far——

HSIEH. ——she is a thousand miles away.

PRECIOUS S. Yes. And if you look near——

HSIEH. ——she is before me. Am I speaking to Mrs. Hsieh, the famous daughter of the Prime Minister Wang?

PRECIOUS S. Oh, no, not the famous, but only the humble wife of Hsieh Ping-Kuei.

HSIEH (*bowing*). My respects to you.

PRECIOUS S. (*curtsying*). You have already paid your respects.

HSIEH. Over-politeness does no harm.

PRECIOUS S. Well said. Now, my husband's letter, please.

HSIEH. One moment. Will you excuse me a minute?

PRECIOUS S.   Certainly.

(*Crosses U.R. to get tea from* PROPERTY MAN.)

HSIEH (*crosses to audience*).   Wait a moment! I was married to her for only a month, and I have been absent from home for eighteen years. I don't know what kind of a woman she really is. Let me try to flirt with her. If she proves to be a good and virtuous woman, I'll tell her who I am and we'll be happily re-united. But if she proves to be a woman of easy virtue, I'll disown her and go back to the Royal Princess of the Western Regions.

(*Crosses to L.C.* PRECIOUS STREAM *crosses to R.C.*)

Ah! Where on earth is that letter?

PRECIOUS S.   Where is it?

HSIEH.   It is lost, madam.

PRECIOUS S.   Don't you know that a letter from one who loves you is worth all the money in the world! You should remember our sage said: 'I examine myself three times every day to see whether I have done truly and loyally my best to my friend.' And you have lost the letter of your friend. I am heart-broken!

HSIEH.   Don't take it so seriously, madam. If you're so anxious about that letter, I'll tell you something I remember that is in it.

PRECIOUS S.   Please tell me what you do remember.

HSIEH.   Listen carefully. 'On the mid-autumn night, under the bright moonlight, Hsieh Ping-Kuei presents his compliments to his dear wife. . . .'

PRECIOUS S.   And mine to him. How has he been lately?

HSIEH.   Very well.

PRECIOUS S.   Safe and sound?

HSIEH.   Safe and sound.

PRECIOUS S.   How about his meals?

HSIEH.   They were badly cooked by the soldiers.

PRECIOUS S. How about his clothes?

HSIEH. He has had to wash and mend them himself. '. . . and begs to tell her that he has been very unfortunate lately. He has suffered severe torture. . . .'

PRECIOUS S. Ah, torture! He was beaten?

HSIEH. Yes, madam, beaten.

PRECIOUS S. How many strokes did he receive?

HSIEH. Forty strokes in all.

PRECIOUS S. Oh, my poor husband.

HSIEH. Don't cry, madam. There are still worse things coming. 'The other day a horse under his care was lost.'

PRECIOUS S. Was it a Government horse or a privately-owned one?

HSIEH. How can there be any privately-owned horses in a camp? Of course it was a Government one.

PRECIOUS S. That being so I suppose he will have to pay for it.

HSIEH. How can he avoid paying for it?

PRECIOUS S. But where can he find the money to pay for it?

HSIEH. He is sure to be able to find the money in some way or other. 'And because of having to pay for the horse, he has had to borrow ten pieces of silver' (*Pointing to himself*). Borrowed from me!

(*Moves nearer her.*)

PRECIOUS S. Stop! Allow me to ask you, what is your rank?

(*Forces him L. one step.*)

HSIEH. I am a captain.

PRECIOUS S. (*another step L.*). And my husband, Hsieh Ping-Kuei?

HSIEH. Also a captain.

PRECIOUS S. (*two steps L.*) If you're both captains, you should get the same amount of pay, then how could you be able to lend him money whilst he had none?

HSIEH. Oh, there is a reason, madam! My eldest brother, Hsieh Ping-Kuei, is a born spendthrift, who squanders all his pay, whilst I, having been born in a humble family, have been accustomed to save all I get. In this way I was able to lend him the money to pay for the horse.

PRECIOUS S. That is not true. My husband was also born in a humble family, and he wouldn't know how to spend his money even if he tried.

(*Crosses D.R.C.*)

HSIEH (*laughing*). Ha, ha!

PRECIOUS S. Oh, dear, he is laughing at me!

(*To audience.*)

HSIEH (*crosses to* PRECIOUS STREAM). The other day I went to his camp to demand the money and he said that he has a wife at home called Lady Precious Stream of the Wang family.

PRECIOUS S. (*furious, forces Hsieh one step L.*). Stop! Let me ask you, has Precious Stream ever owed you anything formerly?

HSIEH. No, nothing.

PRECIOUS S. (*another step L.*). Has she borrowed anything from you recently?

HSIEH. No, nothing.

PRECIOUS S. (*one more step L.*) Why should her name be mentioned?

HSIEH (*forces* PRECIOUS STREAM *one step R.*). Well, let me ask you now. As our old proverb says: 'Father's debts——'

PRECIOUS S. '——the son pays.'

HSIEH (*another step R.*). And the husband's debts?

PRECIOUS S. The wife—the wife doesn't care a fig for them.

(Turns her back on him.)

HSIEH. Well said. But the wife has to pay for them in some other way. Having no ready money, my eldest brother Hsieh agreed to sell his wife, and you know, madam, he did not need to be afraid of there being no bidders, so a bargain was immediately made with a certain officer.

PRECIOUS S. And who is this certain officer?

HSIEH. Eh—eh——

(With a smile.)

Do you understand riddles, madam?

PRECIOUS S. Have you the audacity to say that it is you?

HSIEH. Eh—I haven't the audacity, but I have the proof.

PRECIOUS S. What is your proof?

HSIEH. In the form of a marriage contract.

PRECIOUS S. *(to audience).* Oh, cruel! No, I can't believe it!

(To HSIEH.)

Who are the witnesses to the contract!

HSIEH *(tapping forehead and crossing L.).* They are—they are—Su, the Dragon General; Wei, the Tiger General; and Wang Yun, the Prime Minister.

PRECIOUS S. Nonsense! I won't believe it, because they are all my near relatives, and they would certainly not allow my husband to sell me.

(PRECIOUS STREAM doesn't look at HSIEH. HSIEH crosses U.L. and hides.)

Though I am poor, my father is rich. Let me make out how much the capital and interest amount to now and I will send the money to you. I won't detain you now. Good-bye, and wait for the money in the Western Regions.

(PRECIOUS STREAM *crosses U.R. to be stopped by* HSIEH *who has crossed from U.L.*)

HSIEH (*forcing her D.C.*).   No, no!   It took me forty-eight days to travel from the Western Regions to here, and I have come here specially, not for the money but for the beauty!

PRECIOUS S.   If you go on uttering nonsense and insulting me, I'll call for help and have you arrested.

HSIEH.   But you are as good as my wife.

PRECIOUS S.   Oh, what impudence!

HSIEH (*rises on toes with arms outspread and lunges at her*).   I am going to capture you and carry you off to the Western Regions.

PRECIOUS S. (*retreating to D.L.—to audience*).   Oh, I'm frightened.   The man is a beast!   What shall I do?   There is no help within reach.   Let me think!

(*Taps forehead.*)

Ah! I have it.   I'll throw dust in his eyes.

(*To imaginary person off R.*)

Hello, sir!

(*To* HSIEH.)

Some one is coming over there.

HSIEH (*turning R.*   PRECIOUS STREAM *stoops to pick up dust*).   Where?

(*Turns back to* PRECIOUS STREAM.)

PRECIOUS S. (*rising and pretending to throw dust*).   Good-bye!

(*She crosses U.L. and around the stage.*)

HSIEH (*wiping eyes and crossing D.R.*).   Ah, ha!   A virtuous woman indeed!   No use flirting with her.

(*Gets whip from* PROPERTY MAN.)

It's not very far, so I will not ride but walk to my cave to meet her.

(*Crosses to L. and follows* PRECIOUS STREAM.)

PRECIOUS S. It's too bad. He's following me.

HSIEH. I am your husband, Hsieh Ping-Kuei.

(PRECIOUS STREAM *enters cave, bolts door.* PROPERTY MAN L. *places chair with back to audience at D.C. beside her.* HSIEH *stops at L.C.*)

PRECIOUS S. Let me shut the door and bolt it.

HSIEH. Open the door! You are shutting out your own husband.

PRECIOUS S. You said but a short time ago that you were an officer of the same regiment as my husband, and now you are my husband. You are out of your senses.

HSIEH (*kneels down to talk through door.* PRECIOUS STREAM *is kneeling inside door*). Oh, no! Don't you remember, you told me to be present on the second of February when I received the embroidered ball? We were driven out by your father and lived in this cave. Then I shot and killed the man-devouring tiger and was made a captain, joining the Western Punitive Expedition? I came back to tell you the news, I couldn't bear to leave you. Time was pressing, and I had to cut the reins of my horse which you held tightly in your hands. Then we parted, and that was eighteen years ago.

PRECIOUS S. Did you receive my letter?

HSIEH. Oh, yes. That is why I hurried home.

PRECIOUS S. (*rises and peeks out*). Let me look at . . . (*Closes door again*). No. How can you be my husband with such a strange beard? My husband is a very handsome young man.

HSIEH. Thank you, my third sister. But you ought to say, he used to be a handsome young man. Take yourself, for instance, my dear third sister, you're quite different from the young girl who threw the ball from the pavilion. Consult a looking-glass and tell me what you think.

PRECIOUS S. Don't you know there is no looking-glass in the humble cave?

HSIEH. Oh, I forgot! Look into a basin of water, as you always did formerly.

PRECIOUS S. (*crossing R.*) It is a long time now since I looked into a basin of water, not caring how I looked.

(*Kneels.*)

Oh, horrible! I couldn't call myself Precious Stream now!

HSIEH. Now, open the door and let me in.

PRECIOUS S. (*opens door and puts out hand*). Show me the letter first.

HSIEH (*hands letter to her*). Here is the letter.

PRECIOUS S. (*closes door, crosses R.*). Yes, this is the letter. Oh, my heavens!

HSIEH. Then why do you close the door again?

PRECIOUS S. (*kneeling*). I will open the door only on one condition.

HSIEH. What is your condition, please?

PRECIOUS S. A very simple one. I only want you to go backwards one step.

HSIEH (*he takes one step towards footlights*). All right, I have done so.

PRECIOUS S. Another step, please.

HSIEH (*doing so*). All right. Now open the door.

PRECIOUS S. One step more, please.

HSIEH (*his foot dangling beyond the proscenium*). No, I can't! I have come to the end of things!

PRECIOUS S. If you had not come to the end of things, I'm sure you would never have come back to me. And after you had deserted me for eighteen years you insulted me the moment you met me. What is there to live for? I'd rather die than take back such a husband!

HSIEH.   Please don't say that.   I entreat you to forgive me.

PRECIOUS S.   No.

(PROPERTY MAN L. provides a cushion.)

HSIEH.   I entreat you on my knees.

(He drops on R. knee.)

Look.   I am paying you my highest respects in the presence of hundreds.

PRECIOUS S. *(peeking through door).*   No, I won't look at you.   How about your other knee?   I thought you said you were on your knees.

HSIEH.   Oh, I beg your pardon.

(Slaps left knee and puts it down.)

PRECIOUS S.   Ah, that's better.

(Rises, opens door by pulling chair which is removed by PROPERTY MAN L.)

Come in, my dear!

HSIEH *(rising, handing the cushion to PROPERTY MAN L. and enteting).*   Thank you, my dear!

(He circles stage L., climbing the stairs, followed by PRECIOUS STREAM.)

PRECIOUS S.   To what rank have you been promoted after all these years?

(PROPERTY MAN L. places chair U.C. and stool to its L.)

HSIEH.   Eh?   When your husband has returned from thousands of miles away, the first question you put to him is not about his health, nor his requiring food and drink, but about his rank.   What is rank compared to food and drink?

(He sits in chair.)

PRECIOUS S. *(sits on stool).*   I haven't been very frequently in touch with food and drink during these eighteen years, so I am liable to forget them.

HSIEH. What do you mean? Do you mean to tell me that you haven't had enough to eat and drink during my absence? I remember having made a handsome provision for you just before my departure.

PRECIOUS S. What was it?

HSIEH. Ten hundredweight of firewood and five hundredweight of rice.

PRECIOUS S. Ten hundredweight of firewood and five hundredweight of rice? Even presuming they had everlasting qualities, how could they possibly outlast the wear and tear of all these eighteen years?

HSIEH. Granted. But you ought to have gone to your father and brother-in-law Wei for additional supplies.

PRECIOUS S. They said that your pay had ceased, and offered to make me a loan, which I refused.

HSIEH (*rising*). Splendid! Good-bye!

PRECIOUS S. (*rising*). Where are you going?

HSIEH. To his Excellency, the Prime Minister's house.

PRECIOUS S. (*crossing to R. of* HSIEH). Don't go. My father is not very well.

HSIEH. What is the matter with him?

(PROPERTY MAN *removes chair and stool.*)

PRECIOUS S. The common sickness of great men who don't like to see their poor relatives.

HSIEH. It doesn't matter. I haven't that kind of sickness, and I will condescend to see him.

PRECIOUS S. What are you talking about? *You* condescend to see His Excellency the Prime Minister?

HSIEH. Yes, we have to sometimes.

PRECIOUS S. What do you mean? The King is the only man in the world he would serve.

HSIEH. But I have not said that I am not a King.

PRECIOUS S. *You* a king?

HSIEH.   Yes—only the King of the Western Regions.

PRECIOUS S.   Only the King of the Western Regions!

(*To audience.*)

This seems incredible.

(*To* HSIEH.)

What proof have you?

HSIEH.   What proof do you want?

PRECIOUS S.   Show me your royal seal.

HSIEH.   Nonsense! Whoever heard of any one having asked a king to prove himself a king by showing his royal seal?

PRECIOUS S.   I have never seen a royal seal, and I want very much to see one. Show it to me.

HSIEH.   All right. If I have the royal seal. . . .

PRECIOUS S.   Show it to me and I will believe you are a king.

HSIEH.   And if I haven't the royal seal. . . .

PRECIOUS S.   Then seal your lips so that you will utter no more nonsense.

HSIEH.   Do you really want to see the royal seal?

PRECIOUS S.   Very much.

HSIEH (*paces L. a few steps*). Then let me adjust my hat and dust my jacket.

(PROPERTY MAN L. *hands him seal.*)

Here is the seal of the King of the Western Regions.

PRECIOUS S.   Oh, indeed! The royal seal of the King of the Western Regions! I must kneel down and ask your Majesty's favour.

(PROPERTY MAN R. *provides a cushion.*)

HSIEH (*returns seal to* PROPERTY MAN). Who is she that kneels before me?

PRECIOUS S.   She is Your Majesty's humble maid, Precious Stream.

HSIEH. And for what purpose have you come?

PRECIOUS S. To seek Your Majesty's favour.

HSIEH. You used very harsh and impolite words to me when you addressed me on the spot not far from the cave. I will not bestow on you any favour.

PRECIOUS S. Your humble maid did not know it was Your Majesty then.

HSIEH. If you had known then, you would not have used such harsh and impolite words, would you?

PRECIOUS S. Had she known then, she would have used more harsh and more impolite words.

HSIEH. Indeed! That settles the matter. No favours at all.

PRECIOUS S. (*rising and throwing the cushion to* PROPERTY MAN R.). Then now she must use the most harsh and the most impolite words. Wretch that thou art!

(*Shakes finger at him.*)

HSIEH (*covering ears with hands*). Speak no more! I am about to bestow on you some favour. Hear me!

PRECIOUS S. Yes, Your Majesty.

(*Kneels.* PROPERTY MAN L. *gives her a cushion and* HSIEH *a sword.*)

HSIEH. By the order of His Majesty the King of the Western Regions, Lady Precious Stream of the Wang family is to be crowned Her Majesty.

(*He taps her on back with sword.*)

Queen of the Western Regions.

PRECIOUS S. (*rising and giving* PROPERTY MAN L. *the cushion*). Thanks, Your Majesty.

(*Crosses D.C. to audience—sighs.*)

At last!

HSIEH (*returns sword to* PROPERTY MAN, *crosses to* PRECIOUS

STREAM).   I have been neglecting you all these eighteen years.

PRECIOUS S.   And I have been thinking of you all the time.

HSIEH.   Aren't you glad we are at last united?

PRECIOUS S.   Yes, but I'm afraid it is only a dream. Please pinch me to make sure.

HSIEH.   Nonsense!   Can't you see the bright sun shining? You're not dreaming.

PRECIOUS S.   I'm not dreaming.   I'm not dreaming!

HSIEH.   No!

(*Tries to kiss her right hand.   She takes it away.   Curtsy and bow.*)

Let us retire!   My Queen!

(MUSIC *starts.   They exit L.*   MUSIC *stops.*   LIGHTS *fade.*)

END OF ACT III

(*No Curtain.*)

(Follows immediately—no pause.)

ACT IV

(GONG NO. 1.—*Enter* READER *L.* SPOT *on* READER.)

HONOURABLE READER. Early the next morning we once more have the honour of waiting upon His Excellency, the Prime Minister Wang, at his house. It happens to be his sixtieth birthday, an occasion indeed worthy of celebration. His Excellency gives a magnificent banquet to which nearly everybody of importance is invited. He also gives a special family party in his garden with which we are very pleased to renew our acquaintance. Perhaps it is because we hate the sight of hundreds of intoxicated people drinking toasts and paying compliments to each other in loud tones that sound like quarrelling that we slip out of the big banquet hall unobserved and steal into the garden seeking for tranquillity in spite of our not being members of the family.

The Prime Minister is still the same old obstinate man, quite unchanged after these long years, except the colour of his beard, now assuming a silver grey. He is probably bored by the numerous congratulations he has received from his many guests, and following our example, steals to the garden in search of a little peace. But, unluckily he is to have some unexpected shocks very soon.

(*Exit* READER *L.* GONG NO. 2—LIGHTS *up. Enter* PROPERTY MEN L. *and* R. GONG NO. 3—MUSIC *starts. Enter* ATTENDANTS *and* WANG. TWO ATTENDANTS *enter* R., *cross to D.L. and D.R.* WANG *enters R. down to C.* MUSIC *stops.*)

WANG. To be the Prime Minister is to be second to none and above all other officers! To most people my post is a very enviable one, yet as one who has had more than enough of it, I regard it as scarcely worth all the trouble it gives.

(PROPERTY MAN R. *places arm-chair C.*)

If you are unpopular you receive all the bricks—

(*Up C. and sits.*)

and if you are popular, you receive endless congratulations which is even worse.

(PROPERTY MAN L. *gets table from up L. puts it before* WANG.)

A famous statesman is like a famous actor, everybody wants to pat him on the back, and you must have at least a dozen secretaries to pick out the letters of your real friends from the thousands of others from people you don't know. The worst of all is your birthday. Once a year you must let thousands of people congratulate you on a matter which was no doing of yours. If there is another congratulatory ceremony I shall go mad!

ATTENDANTS (*kneeling*). We beg to report to Your Excellency——

WANG. What?

ATTENDANTS. That the Right Honourable gentlemen of the Cabinet present their compliments to you and——

ATTENDANTS and WANG (*together*). Come to congratulate you (me) on your sixtieth birthday.

WANG. To the pit of hell with them!

ATTENDANTS (*rising*). Yes, Your Excellency.

WANG. No, no, to the seats of honour with them, and say that I regret I can't receive them in person for I am not well—not at all well. I will thank them for their kindness—I shall have to say their kindness—to-morrow when we meet in court.

ATTENDANTS. Yes, Excellency.

WANG. I will kill the next one who comes.

ATTENDANTS (*kneeling*). We beg to report to Your Excellency——

WANG (*rises*).   What?

ATTENDANTS.   ——that Lady Precious Stream has come to pay her respects to Your Excellency.

WANG.   Show her in.

(*Sits.*)

ATTENDANTS.   Yes, Excellency.

(*Cross U.L. and U.R., turn R.*)

Show Lady Precious Stream in, please.

PRECIOUS S. (*offstage*).   I am coming.

(MUSIC *starts.   She enters to C.*   MUSIC *stops.*)

Eighteen years have passed since I was last at the Prime Minister's house, which is now newly painted and beautifully decorated, and quite different from what it used to be.

(*Moves slightly L.   Turns.*)

Well, here is the garden at last.

(ATTENDANTS *return to places.*   PROPERTY MAN L. *puts cushion for* PRECIOUS STREAM *to kneel on.   Up C. kneels before* WANG.)

The unfilial daughter, Precious Stream, presents her respects to her father.

WANG (*rises.   Peers over table*).   You—Precious Stream?

PRECIOUS S.   Yes, Your Excellency?

WANG.   Oh, my dear daughter!

PRECIOUS S.   Oh, my dear father!

WANG.   Not having seen her for eighteen years, I cannot restrain the tears from flowing from my eyes the moment that we meet.

(PROPERTY MAN L. *puts chair L. of table for* PRECIOUS STREAM.   *When* PRECIOUS STREAM *rises she hands cushion to* PROPERTY MAN L.)

I wonder what has made her come to my house? Don't stand on ceremony, my child.   Be seated.

(She rises and sits L. of WANG.)

PRECIOUS S. Thank you. How have you been lately, my father?

WANG. I have been very well. Now, my child, what has made you come to my house?

PRECIOUS S. To congratulate you on your birthday, dear father.

WANG. Oh! Why should you remember my birthday when you have no wish to remember me?

PRECIOUS S. There are things which one cannot forget even if one tries.

WANG *(in a temper).* Yes! yes!

(Calms down.)

No! no! Go to the inner chamber to see your mother.

PRECIOUS S. *(rises).* Yes, your orders will be obeyed.

(PROPERTY MAN L. *removes* PRECIOUS STREAM'S *chair. Crosses D.L.C. to audience.)*

My father is still annoyed with me, and does not wish to speak to me. I now go to the inner chamber to see my dear mother.

(Exits L.)

ATTENDANTS *(kneeling).* We beg to report to Your Excellency——

WANG. What!

ATTENDANTS. ——that your two sons-in-law, the great Dragon General and the great Tiger General—

(WANG *rises and glares at them. Whispering as they rise.)*

have come to congratulate you on your sixtieth birthday.

WANG. Show them in!

ATTENDANTS. Yes, Excellency.

(Cross up and call.)

Show the Generals in, please.

(MUSIC *starts. Enter* SU *and* WEI *down R., to C.,* bow to *audience, then up C. to* WANG. *Bow before him.* MUSIC *stops.*)

SU and WEI.   How are you, my dear father-in-law?

WANG.   Much as usual, thanks!   Be seated!

(*He waves them to seats R. of him.   They sit.* SU *next to him;* WEI *R. of* SU. ATTENDANTS *return to places.*)

Now, my two excellent sons-in-law, don't tell me that you have come to my house to congratulate me on my birthday.

SU and WEI.   That is exactly what we have come for.

WANG (*deep sigh*).   My heavens!   Now let us talk about something else.   Do you know that we have a rare visitor here to-day?

SU and WEI.   No, dear father-in-law.

WANG.   And that is the great difference between this and past years, it is an occasion worthy of celebration.

SU and WEI.   Why?

WANG.   My third daughter has come back to me at last

SU and WEI.   Who?

WANG.   Precious Stream, my third daughter.   Don't you remember her?

SU and WEI.   Oh, yes!

(*They both nod to* WANG.)

Of course!

(*They nod to each other.*)

WANG.   She has come back to me at last.

WEI.   Ah ha!   Now, old Su, I feel sure that our third sister-in-law is tired of her lonely life in her cave, and has come back to find a second husband.   We live and we learn.

SU.   We live, it is true, but learn nothing.

WANG.   Attendants!

ATTENDANTS (*kneeling*).   Yes, Excellency!

WANG.   Request madam and the three young ladies to come here.

ATTENDANTS.   Yes, Excellency.

            (*Cross upstage and call:*)

Show in Madam and the three ladies.

LADIES (*offstage*).   Yes, we are coming.

    (MUSIC *starts.* MADAM, SILVER STREAM, GOLDEN STREAM *and* PRECIOUS STREAM *enter R. come downstage, speak to audience, preceded by* 1ST *and* 2ND MAIDS. MUSIC *stops.*)

MADAM.   Lofty and majestic is our house.

        (*Up C. to* WANG. *Sits on his left.*)

GOLDEN S.   With gold and silver us heaven endows.

      (*Up C. Curtsies to* WANG. *Sits next to* MADAM.)

SILVER S.   Handsome and noble is my spouse.

PRECIOUS S.   But poor am I as a church mouse.

    (*Curtsies, sit in end chair L.* MAIDS *cross upstage and behind* MADAM.)

WANG.   Attendants!

ATTENDANTS (*kneeling*).   Yes, Excellency.

WANG.   Serve the wine at once.

ATTENDANTS (*rising*).   Yes, Excellency.

    (MUSIC *starts.* ATTENDANTS *place wine on table.* WANG *pours out wine.* MUSIC *softer.*)

WANG.   Drink, my dear sons-in-law.

                (*All rise.*)

SU and WEI.   Thank you, dear father-in-law.

ALL.   Here's to you, father.

    (MUSIC *loud.* WANG *shakes jug, pours out for himself only.* MUSIC *softer.*)

WANG. Here's to the whole family.

(*He drinks.* MUSIC *loud.*)

ALL. Thank you.

(*All sit.* ATTENDANT R. *removes tray and gives it to* PROPERTY MAN R. PROPERTY MAN L. *moves table to up L.* MUSIC *stops.* ATTENDANTS *retire to U.L. and U.R.*)

WANG. Now, Precious Stream——

PRECIOUS S. Yes, Your Excellency.

(*Stands, curtsies.*)

WANG. My dear daughter.

PRECIOUS S. My dear father.

(*Sits.*)

WANG. I have something to say to you, but I don't know whether I ought to say it during this feast.

PRECIOUS S. A father's advice to his daughter is welcome at any time.

WANG. As your husband died in the Western Regions years ago, I, being your father, naturally am worried about you. I have a mind to choose, among the younger members of my Cabinet, a suitable husband for you. As I am getting old, I wish to have a son-in-law to live with me. What do you think of that, my child?

PRECIOUS S. Oh, no, father. Even if my husband is dead, which I have good reason to believe is not the case, I should remain a widow and be faithful to his memory.

WANG. My dear child, you know nothing about life! The old proverbs say: 'To remain a widow and be faithful to your husband's memory is easily said, but difficult to carry out to the end.' If you can't carry out your words loyally to the end you will become the laughing-stock of every one!

PRECIOUS S. I think the old proverb is as you say: 'To

remain a widow and be faithful to your husband's memory is easily said but difficult to carry out to the end.' If you can't carry it out to the end, that is none of your father's business.

WANG. Silence, you little wretch! I'd rather see you damned than the laughing-stock of every one.

MADAM. Don't mind what your father says, dear.

WANG. You old baggage! You have utterly spoiled her.

MADAM. Do as you think best, and you'll have all my blessings.

GOLDEN S. And my good wishes, too.

PRECIOUS S. Thank you.

WANG. Now, my excellent sons-in-law, will you try to say something to her for me!

SU. No, my dear father-in-law, I don't think it would be any use.

WEI. Let me go to her, and before I have said half a dozen words, she is sure to consent to marry again.

(Rises and crosses D.C. to audience.)

I will give her one of my most charming smiles.

(Pulls beard away from mouth and smiles at audience.)

One hundred forms of ugliness is hidden by a smile.

(Crosses to L. of PRECIOUS STREAM.*)*

My dear sister-in-law, your father's suggestion that you should marry again is a very considerate one. I would like you to think it over carefully for your own sake.

(Smile business to PRECIOUS STREAM.*)*

PRECIOUS S. Who is this man swaying to and fro before me?

WEI. Don't you recognize my musical voice and know that I am your brother-in-law Wei.

PRECIOUS S. Have you the audacity to tell me you are Wei, the Tiger General.

WEI. Yes, your brother-in-law, the famous Tiger General.

PRECIOUS S. What is your business here?

WEI. Eh—eh——·

PRECIOUS S. Have you the insolence to try to persuade me to marry again?

WEI. Well . . .

PRECIOUS S. How dare you speak of such a thing to me? The day you are under my thumb, you shall pay for this!

WEI. Nonsense and stuff.

(Crosses D.C. to audience.)

Stuff and nonsense.

(Crosses back to his chair.)

ALL. Well?

WEI. We—l—ll.

(Sits.)

SILVER S. *(Rises, crosses R., then back to PRECIOUS STREAM).* Excuse me for a minute, please.

WEI. Where are you going with your mincing gait?

SILVER S. To try and persuade my sister to re-marry.

WEI *(fiercely).* Sit down!

(Sweetly.)

Dear.

(She curtsies and sits.)

WANG. Precious Stream seems to be very self-possessed to-day. It may be true that her husband, Hsieh Ping-Kuei, is still alive.

SU. Yes, I think he is. I think he is.

GOLDEN S. And I think so, too.

WANG. It would be a good thing to have him dead.

MADAM. No, better to have him alive.

WEI. Better to have him dead.

SILVER S. Better to have him alive—dead.

SU and GOLDEN S. No, better to have him alive.

WEI. No, better to have him dead, definitely dead.

(GONG.)

VOICE (*off R.*). Prepare yourselves to receive the Imperial Edict from His Majesty the Emperor of China.

(GONG. *All rise, cross down, kneel on cushions placed in a row by* PROPERTY MEN. MAIDS *and* ATTENDANTS *in row behind.*)

His Imperial Majesty orders the Prime Minister Wang to welcome His Majesty, Hsieh Ping-Kuei, King of the Western Regions, to his court to-morrow, and bring Wei, the Tiger General, with him under arrest. Long live the Emperor!

(GONG.)

ALL. We hear and we obey! Long live the Emperor!

(GONG. ALL *rise looking at* PRECIOUS STREAM. PROPERTY MEN *collect cushions that* ALL *hold behind them.*)

Hsieh Ping-Kuei? King of the Western Regions?

(ATTENDANTS *cross to* WEI *and take him prisoner.*)

WANG (*going L.*). Good heavens! What shall I do? What shall I do?

MADAM (*following*). You always know what to do.

WANG (*angrily*). Of course I know. I am not speaking to you, I am addressing the audience.

(*Exeunt.* MAIDS *follow and exit.* SU *and* GOLDEN STREAM *follow and exit.*)

WEI (*looking at* PRECIOUS STREAM). I crave your pardon, Your Majesty.

(PRECIOUS STREAM *laughs and exits.*)

WEI (*being escorted out by* ATTENDANTS). I am a dead man! I am a dead man!

SILVER S. (*crossing D.C. to audience.*) I am indeed as good as a widow already. Very silly indeed! I don't like this act at all.

(MUSIC *starts.* SILVER STREAM *exits* L. MUSIC *stops.* LIGHTS *fade.* GONG NO. 1—*Enter* READER L. SPOT *on* READER.)

HONOURABLE READER. We have now the honour of being present at the temporary court of His Majesty the King of the Western Regions during his visit to China. It is one of the most beautiful buildings in the Chinese Kingdom, and is specially decorated to welcome its royal occupant. The onlookers have to suppose that rich silk canopies hang over their heads and soft carpets are under their feet, and that the furniture is all of ebony, though what they actually see is still the same old stage without any alteration.

The patient audience is requested not to be alarmed when the author is compelled to bring in a new character at this late hour of the evening (afternoon), because without him the author himself would be forced to pay the penalty of marrying a desirable yet undesirable Western lady. The solution of this problem is in the person of His Excellency the Minister of Foreign Affairs, a man of the world who must have had many affairs in foreign countries. By this arrangement the performance will speedily come to a satisfactory conclusion, which will enable our patrons to get home before (soon after) eleven (five), and will prove that the Chinese play is no longer than a Western one, seldom longer than *Hamlet,* and never longer than *Back to Methusalah.*

(*Exit* READER L. GONG NO. 2—LIGHTS *up.* GONG NO. 3—MUSIC *starts. Enter* ATTENDANTS *followed by* HSIEH. ATTENDANTS *go to* D.R. *and* D.L. HSIEH *to* D.C. MUSIC *stops.* PROPERTY MEN R. *place arm-chair* C.)

HSIEH. I left here no more than a beggar, and have returned as a King. Let me sit on my throne.

(*Crosses U.C. sits.*)

As I came here from the Imperial Palace all the streets were filled with people who kept on scattering flowers upon me. If they had only shown me even the very slightest degree of similar enthusiasm eighteen years ago when I was performing my best feats of strength in those very streets, they would have made me a much happier man! Their cheers are now to me quite distasteful! My only happiness is the company of my Queen!

(*He calls.*)

Attendants!

ATTENDANTS. Yes, Your Masjety.

HSIEH. Request Her Majesty the Queen to come to Court.

ATTENDANTS. Yes, Your Majesty.

(ATTENDANTS *both cross upstage and face R.*)

His Majesty requests the presence of Her Majesty, the Queen.

PRECIOUS S. (*offstage*). To hear is to obey.

(MUSIC *starts. She enters R. preceded by four* MAIDS, *who go R. and L. She to C.*)

After wearing rags for eighteen years, I now have the joy of being arrayed in royal robes.

(PROPERTY MAN L. *places chair for* LADY PRECIOUS STREAM. *Up C. before* HSIEH.)

Your humble wife presents her respects to Your Majesty.

HSIEH (*standing*). Thank you. Don't stand on ceremony. Please be seated.

PRECIOUS S. Thank you for your condescension.

(*She sits on his L.* MAIDS *upstage R. and L. behind C. chair*).

May I ask how Your Majesty got on this morning at your reception at the Emperor's Court?

HSIEH. The reception was a great success. The Emperor has ordered the prisoner Wei to be placed at my disposal.

PRECIOUS S. Splendid! What has Your Majesty done with him?

HSIEH. Nothing yet. I want you to decide for me.

PRECIOUS S. Very good. Have him brought here.

HSIEH. Attendants! Order them to bring the prisoner Wei here at once.

ATTENDANTS. Yes, Your Majesty.

(Both cross upstage and face R.)

Bring the prisoner Wei here at once.

EXECUTIONER'S VOICE *(offstage)*. Without delay.

(PROPERTY MAN R. puts cushion C. near footlights for WEI to kneel on. WEI enters R. with handcuffs on, comes down C. kneels, facing audience. EXECUTIONER is R. of him, with sword.)

WEI. When I heard that I was wanted here, I became almost senseless. The prisoner Wei awaits Your Majesty's pleasure.

HSIEH. Who is kneeling before me?

WEI. The prisoner Wei.

HSIEH. Do you confess that you plotted to kill me during the Western Punitive Expedition?

WEI. I confess. I only crave your pardon, Your Majesty.

PRECIOUS S. Do you confess that you have been swindling me out of what was due me in order to starve me to death?

WEI. I confess. I only crave your pardon, my dear sister—er—Your Majesty.

PRECIOUS S. How can you be pardoned? No, you will not be pardoned.

HSIEH. No, you will not be pardoned. Therefore the penalty of your crime——

PRECIOUS S. Of your numerous crimes——

HSIEH. Yes, the penalty of your numerous crimes is—
(*Looks at his wife, who touches her throat with her sleeve.*)
is death.

WEI. Oh, no!
(*Bows down.*)

HSIEH. Executioner!

EXECUTIONER. Yes, Your Majesty!

HSIEH. Behead the prisoner!

EXECUTIONER. Yes, Your Majesty!

(EXECUTIONER *puts sword against* WEI'S *neck and starts to swing.*)

SILVER S. (*offstage*). Please; Executioner, wait a moment.

(WEI *rises, goes* L., *followed by* EXECUTIONER. SILVER STREAM *enters and comes* C. *and addresses audience.*)

Oh, I am so glad I have come in time.
(*Curtsies.*)

I will ask my brother-in-law for his pardon. I have heard people say that many lives have been saved only through wives arriving in the nick of time.
(*Giggles to audience.*)

WEI (*kneeling at* L.). Please don't waste your time in coquetting with the audience, but go in and ask for pardon at once.

(SILVER STREAM *goes* L. *of* WEI. PROPERTY MAN L. *puts cushion* C. *for* SILVER STREAM *to kneel on.*)

SILVER S. You horrid wretch, you deserve death.
(*Up* C. *kneels before* HSIEH.)

My respects to Your Majesty, my dear brother-in-law.

HSIEH. Who is kneeling before me?

SILVER S. Your Majesty's sister-in-law, Silver Stream.

HSIEH. What have you come here for?

SILVER S. To ask for my husband's pardon.

(HSIEH *looks at his wife, who signs to him not to do so.*)

HSIEH. No, you have both behaved very badly to us. I cannot pardon him.

SILVER S. (*rises and hands cushion to* PROPERTY MAN L.). Nothing can be done now.

WEI. You have come in time only to see me die.

SILVER S. Let me call for help.

(*She goes up L. round stage and exits R.*)

EXECUTIONER (*sharpens sword on footlights*). Let me finish my job. The sooner the better.

(*Starts to swing.*)

SILVER S. (*offstage*). Executioner, pray wait a minute.

(SILVER STREAM *enters R., pushing* WANG *in front of her.*) Quick, father. His Excellency the Prime Minister Wang is here.

(WANG *enters to D.R.*)

2ND ATTENDANT R. I beg to report to Your Majesty that His Excellency the Prime Minister Wang is here.

(HSIEH *looks at his wife who shakes her head.*)

HSIEH. Tell His Excellency that I can't grant him an audience at present, but if he will wait a few hours, I may give him a few seconds then.

ATTENDANT. Yes, Your Majesty.

SILVER S. (*Down C.*). This is no good. I must try again. (*Goes up L. round back of stage and exits R.*)

ATTENDANT (*to* WANG). His Majesty regrets that he can't grant you an audience at present, and says if you will wait a few hours His Majesty may be able to give you a few seconds then.

WANG. Oh, my God!

(*He faints in the arms of* PROPERTY MEN.)

EXECUTIONER. Now for it!

(*Starts to swing sword.*)

SILVER S. (*offstage*).   Executioner, do wait a second!
(*Enters to D.R.*)

Oh, quick, it's a matter of life and death.   His Honour
General Su and his wife are coming.

ATTENDANT.   I beg to report to Your Majesty that His
Honour General Su and his wife are coming.

(SU *and his* WIFE *enter to D.R.*)

HSIEH.   Tell His Honour General Su and his wife that
I shall be very glad to receive them if they promise
not to refer in any way to the prisoner who is to be
executed.

ATTENDANT.   Yes, Your Majesty.

SILVER S. (*C.*)   Heaven have mercy on me.   I have been
running to and fro in vain.   There is still one more
chance.

(*Crosses upstage, round back of it—and exits R.*)

ATTENDANT (*to* SU).   His Majesty says he will be very
glad to receive you if you mention nothing about the
prisoner who is to be executed.

SU *and* GOLDEN STREAM (*cross to* WEI *and* EXECUTIONER).
That's very hard!   We have come specially on his
account.

(*They face C.*)

EXECUTIONER.   I am sorry.   I can't wait any longer.
(*Starts to swing.*)

SILVER S. (*offstage*).   Executioner, do wait a little.

(SILVER STREAM *enters to D.R.*)

Quick, mother!   You are my last hope.   Madam is
coming.

(MADAM *enters to R.C.*)

ATTENDANT.   I beg to report to Your Majesty that Madam
your mother-in-law, is coming.

HSIEH (*rising*).   All right.   We must rise to welcome her.
(*Bows.*)   My respects to you, my dear mother-in-law

PRECIOUS S. (*curtsies*). My respects, dear mother.

MADAM. Don't stand on ceremony, dear children.

(*Sees* WANG.)

What are you sitting there for, my dear?

WANG (*who has been on floor since his faint*). I was told to wait here for a few hours before he could see me for a few seconds.

MADAM (*laughs*). Serves you right.

(*Turns L., sees* SU *and* GOLDEN STREAM.)

What are you here for, my children?

(PROPERTY MEN *pick up* WANG.)

SU. We came to ask them to pardon Wei.

GOLDEN S. But His Majesty forbade us to mention anything about the prisoner.

(PROPERTY MAN R. *puts chair R. of* HSIEH. PROPERTY MAN L. *puts two chairs L. of* PRECIOUS STREAM.)

MADAM. Oh, so that's it, is it?

(*Taps forehead with fingers.*)

Of course we mustn't mention the prisoner to His Majesty.

SILVER S. But you——

MADAM. Foolish child! Come with me, all of you.

(*All cross to in front of* HSIEH.)

HSIEH (*rising*). Be seated.

(*All sit.*)

MADAM. And now let me have His Majesty's word of honour that he will not mention even the name of the prisoner Wei.

HSIEH. I gladly give you my word.

SILVER S. But you said you would not mention about my husband to His Majesty.

MADAM. Certainly. I give him my word of honour, too.

(To HSIEH.)

Isn't that fair?

HSIEH. Oh, quite fair.

SILVER S. Oh, mother, how can you!

MADAM. Silence! Don't let me hear you speak again.

PRECIOUS S. Mother, darling, you are full of understanding.

MADAM. Am I? I want you to grant me a favour, and I hope you will show me how full you are of understanding.

PRECIOUS S. Of course I will. Before you say the word, your request is granted.

MADAM. That is very kind of you.

(Rises and curtsies before PRECIOUS STREAM.)

And I must thank Your Majesty formally for your favour.

(All rise).

PRECIOUS S. Please don't, mother.

(All sit.)

What is it?

MADAM. I want you to pardon Wei.

PRECIOUS S. But you have given your word of honour that you would never mention him.

MADAM. Yes, to His Majesty, not to Her Majesty.

HSIEH *(rising)*. But he deserves more than death.

(All rise.)

MADAM. No, remember your word and don't mention the prisoner to me, Your Majesty.

HSIEH *(sitting)*. Well, I'm . . .

(All sit.)

MADAM. Since Her Majesty has granted my request——

PRECIOUS S. No, I have not.

MADAM.   Yes, you have.   Everybody understood that you had granted it before I told you what it was, and I thanked you formally for your favour.

(*All nod.*)

PRECIOUS S.   Well, even if I promised you, I'm afraid my husband won't listen to me.

HSIEH.   No, I won't.

MADAM.   But you must; in this and every other kingdom all the best families are ruled by the wife.   My husband here will tell you that he always listened to me and he will always have to listen to me.   He will set you a good example, won't you, my dear?

WANG.   Eh—ah—yes.

MADAM.   And willingly?

WANG.   Willingly.

PRECIOUS S.   Dear mother, you are indeed a darling.   As I have already promised my mother, I'm afraid you will have to fulfil my promise.

HSIEH.   I said it was for you to decide.

PRECIOUS S.   Splendid!

ALL.   Splendid!

PRECIOUS S.   His life may be spared.

WEI (*looking up*).   Ah!

PRECIOUS S.   But he must be punished in some other way.

WEI (*bowing down*).   Oh!

PRECIOUS S.   I think a few strokes on his back might meet the case.

SILVER S.   Yes, I too think that he ought to be beaten, for he has behaved very badly to me.

PRECIOUS S.   Yes, he really deserves to be beaten severely.

WEI.   Oh, no, I'd rather die; I'd rather die!

(*He grabs sword and places it at his neck.*   EXECUTIONER *swings, but* WEI *ducks just in time.*)

HSIEH. Attendants!

ATTENDANT. Yes, Your Majesty.

HSIEH. Release the prisoner, and bring him here to be beaten.

ATTENDANT. Yes, Your Majesty.

EXECUTIONER (*throws sword on the ground*). Bad luck! I have been deprived of my diversion to-day.

(*He exits L. ATTENDANTS come forward and WEI C. before HSIEH. ATTENDANT L. takes the handcuffs and gives them to PROPERTY MAN L. PROPERTY MAN R. places cushion C. for WEI to kneel, PROPERTY MAN L. picks up sword, takes it L.*)

HSIEH (*looks at his wife—she holds up four fingers.*) Give him four hundred strokes on the back.

ATTENDANT. Yes, Your Majesty.

(*PROPERTY MAN L. gives ATTENDANT stick. PROPERTY MAN R. ditto. L. ATTENDANT holds stick in front of WEI'S back.*)

WEI. I shall be a dead man long before they've finished.

HSIEH. Beat him!

PRECIOUS S. Stop! Forty strokes will be enough.

HSIEH. All right, forty strokes.

ATTENDANTS (*together*). Yes, Your Majesty.
                    (*Count aloud.*)

   Five!

WEI (*yells*). Ouch!

ATTENDANTS. Ten.

WEI. Ouch!

ATTENDANTS. Fifteen.

WEI. Ouch!

ATTENDANTS. Twenty.

WEI. Ouch!

ATTENDANTS. Twenty-five.

WEI. Ouch!

ATTENDANTS. Thirty.

WEI. Ouch!

ATTENDANTS. Thirty-five.

WEI. Ouch!

ATTENDANTS. Forty.

WEI. Ouch!

ATTENDANTS. We have given him forty strokes, Your Majesty.

HSIEH. You may leave him here.

ATTENDANTS. Yes, Your Majesty.

(*They hand sticks to* PROPERTY MEN *and retire to their places D.R. and D.L.*)

PRECIOUS S. Now let bygones be bygones and take a seat beside your wife.

(WEI *rises.*)

SILVER S. You must thank their Majesties.

(PROPERTY MAN R. *puts chair R. for* WEI *and takes the cushion from the ground to put it on the chair.*)

WEI (*rising*). Oh, thank you indeed! Ouch! Ouch!
(*Goes to chair R., tries to sit, finds it impossible to do so, rises and leans over back of chair.*)

SILVER S. (*rising*). Why don't you sit down? Why do you stand in such a ridiculous position?

WEI. How can I sit down with wounds like mine?

SILVER S. This will keep you from being naughty for a long time.

(*Sits.*)

MADAM. Yes, it will.

(*To* WANG.)

Don't be cross, dear. Aren't you delighted to see all our children happily united?

WANG. I am.

PRECIOUS S. Oh, dear mother, there is a member who
has lately joined our family. You mustn't go before
meeting her.

ALL. Who is she?

PRECIOUS S. My sister-in-law.

(*To* HSIEH.)

Isn't she your sister, dear?

HSIEH (*uncomfortably*). Eh—eh—yes.

MADAM. But we never heard before that you had a sister.

PRECIOUS S. Neither had he until recently. I haven't
even seen her yet.

GOLDEN S. Where is she?

PRECIOUS S. I know that she is awaiting an audience
here.

SILVER S. Request her to come at once, please.

PRECIOUS S. Yes, please.

HSIEH. Attendants!

ATTENDANTS. Yes, Your Majesty.

HSIEH. Request the presence of Her Highness . . .

PRECIOUS S. His sister.

HSIEH. . . . immediately.

ATTENDANTS. Yes, Your Majesty.

(ATTENDANTS *cross upstage, turn R. and call.*)

His Majesty requests the presence of Her Highness, his
sister.

PRINCESS (*offstage*). To hear is to obey.

(MUSIC *starts.* MA TA *and* KIANG HAI *enter R.* *Come down R.L. and L.C.* PRINCESS *to C.* MUSIC *stops.*)

MA TA. I beg to report to Your Highness that this is the Court of His Majesty.

PRINCESS. Indeed!

(*She looks around.*)

What a queer place it is! China is indeed a queer land. Everything is just the opposite to our country. To one who has been born and bred in the Western Regions and accustomed to the freedom there, their punctilious etiquette and strange customs are most trying.

(*She turns and looks at* HSIEH.)

Ma Ta and Kiang Hai!

MA TA *and* KIANG HAI. Yes, Your Highness.

PRINCESS. Who is the man sitting there like the King of Heaven?

MA TA. He is His Majesty our King.

PRINCESS. How changed he is! I'm a little afraid of him and who is that little *goddess* sitting next to His Majesty?

KIANG HAI. The famous Precious Stream of the Wang family. She is his wife.

PRINCESS (*starts L.*) Oh, I can't abide this. Let us go back to the Western Regions.

MA TA *and* KIANG HAI (*stopping her*). Oh, no, we can't.

PRINCESS. What am I to do?

MA TA. You must go to her and salute her.

PRINCESS. I won't salute her.

KIANG HAI. If you don't, they will say that the women of the Western Regions have very bad manners.

PRINCESS. Then I must do it for the reputation of our women.

MA TA and KIANG HAI (*step R. and L. three steps*). Yes, Your Highness.

PRINCESS (*upstage R.C.*). My respects to you, the famous Precious Stream of the Wang family.

(*She gives her a military salute.* PRECIOUS STREAM *raises both hands. Down C.*)

Ma Ta and Kiang Hai!

MA TA and KIANG HAI (*cross in three steps*). Yes, Your Highness?

PRINCESS. Why does she appear to try to fly when I salute her?

MA TA. She isn't flying, she's returning your salute.

PRINCESS. That is not a salute.

KIANG HAI (*saluting*). She's never done this before. Their way of saluting is quite different to ours.

PRINCESS. What is the difference?

MA TA. Our way of saluting is like raising the hand to hit a dog.

(*Salutes.*)

KIANG HAI. Their mode of saluting is like churning cream.

(*Churns cream.*)

PRINCESS (*trying to churn cream*). How ridiculous!

MA TA. They say that the hitting a dog salute is equally, if not more, ridiculous.

PRINCESS. Well, I must try to churn cream in her honour.

MA TA and KIANG HAI (*back three steps*). Yes, Your Highness.

PRINCESS.   Watch me, Ma Ta and Kiang Hai.

> (*She goes up R.C. and churns invisible cream.*)

My respects to you!

> (PRECIOUS STREAM *rises and curtsies.*)

PRECIOUS S.   Many thanks.   Please don't stand on ceremony.

> (*Down C. to audience.*)

How beautiful and charming the Princess is.   I now quite see why my husband didn't return to me earlier. If I were a man, I should like to stay in the Western Regions for a few years, too.   As I'm a woman I hate her!   I do not wish to speak to such a bewitching little minx, but if I do not, she will say that the women of China are very impolite.   For the sake of preserving the reputation of the women in China, I will say a few kind words to her.

> (*She goes up R.C.   During this speech the* PRINCESS *has taken* PRECIOUS STREAM'S *chair next to* HSIEH. *She tries to make advances to him, he practically ignores her.   She smiles at* SU, *who turns his back upon her.   When* PRECIOUS STREAM *comes upstage, she rises and faces her.*)   I am indebted to you for having entertained my husband for me all these eighteen years.

PRINCESS (*aside*).   She is trying to be funny.

> (*To* PRECIOUS STREAM.)

Oh, you needn't be, I was only too delighted to do so.

> (*Churns cream.*)

PRECIOUS S. (*aside*).   The baggage!   This is my father, and this is my mother.

> (*They rise and the* PRINCESS *churns cream to them.*)

And these are my two sisters and two brothers-in-law.

> (PRECIOUS STREAM *sits.*   PRINCESS *moves over to* WEI.)

PRINCESS. But this man seems to have no face.

(*She touches* WEI's *back. He turns.*)

WEI. Ouch! Ouch!

PRINCESS. Oh! Oh! I must go! I must go!

(*She retreats L.*)

PRECIOUS S. Wait a moment, please.

(*Whispers to* HSIEH.)

So and So.

HSIEH. Oh, yes. Attendants! Request So and So to come here immediately.

ATTENDANTS. Yes, Your Majesty.

(ATTENDANTS *turn R. and call.*)

His Majesty requests the presence of So and So.

MINISTER (*off L.*). Coming.

(MUSIC *starts. He enters R. to down C.* MUSIC *stops.*)

Your most obedient humble servant, So and So, the Minister of Foreign Affairs.

(*Turns and bows to* HSIEH.)

My respects to Your Majesty.

HSIEH. Thank you. Don't stand on ceremony. I want to tell you that the Princess of the Western Regions, has arrived here to-day, and hopes you will welcome her and see that she has everything she wants.

MINISTER. Yes, Your Majesty. Delighted, Your Majesty

(*He takes the Princess's outstretched hand and kisses it.*)

My sincere welcome and respect to Your Highness.

(*As he kisses, all turn heads away.*)

PRINCESS. Oh, thank you.

MINISTER (*offering his R. arm*). Will Your Highness come with me?

PRINCESS (*taking his arm*). With pleasure!

MINISTER. Excuse us, Your Majesty. Good morning, everybody.

(*They sweep round stage, then up L.*)

PRINCESS. Good-bye, everybody. Tell me, where did you learn your charming manners, Your Excellency?

MINISTER. In London.

(*Both exit L.*)

WANG (*rising*). Disgraceful!

MADAM (*rising*). Scandalous!

SU and GOLDEN S. (*rising*). Disgusting!

WEI and SILVER S. (*rising*). Shameful!

WANG. This is too much. I think I shall retire.

(PROPERTY MEN R. *and* L. *remove chairs.* WANG *comes down C. bows to audience exits L.* MADAM *follows him, curtsies, says 'Good-bye' to audience and follows him off.* SU *and* GOLDEN STREAM *come down C, bow and curtsy to audience.*)

SU and GOLDEN S. Good-bye, we must go back.

(*Exit L.*)

WEI and SILVER S. Good-bye. Thank you.

(*Exit L. followed by* TWO ATTENDANTS *and by* MAIDS.)

HSIEH (*rises*). Let us retire.

PRECIOUS S. (*she rises*). Do you always behave in the Western Regions as they two were doing? Why not give me a chance?

(*She tries to take his arm.* PROPERTY MEN R. *and* L. *remove the two chairs.*)

HSIEH. For shame!

(*He will not allow her to take her arm. She curtsies.*)

Our affection is for each other, and not for public entertainment.

PRECIOUS S. (*imitating the* MINISTER *and* PRINCESS). My sincere welcome and respects to you, Your Highness.

(HSIEH *commences to walk downstage, round and up L.*)

Oh thank you.

(*She offers her arm.*)

Will Your Highness come with me?   With pleasure!

(*Kisses her hand to audience and exits after* HSIEH *L.*)

CURTAIN

(*End of Play.*)

SUGGESTIONS FOR DOUBLES

ACT I		ACT II	
Scene I	Scene II	Scene I	Scene II
	Reader		Reader
	Property Man		Property Man
	Property Man		Property Man
Wang Yun	Wang Yun		
Madam Wang	Madam Wang		Madam Wang
Su—Dragon General	Su—Dragon General		
Wei—Tiger General	Wei—Tiger General		
Silver Stream	Silver Stream		
Golden Stream	Golden Stream		
Precious Stream	Precious Stream	Precious Stream	Precious Stream
Gardener	Gardener	Gardener	
1st Attendant	1st Attendant		1st Attendant
2nd Attendant	2nd Attendant		2nd Attendant
1st Maid	1st Maid		1st Maid
2nd Maid	2nd Maid		2nd Maid
3rd Maid	3rd Maid		
	4th Maid		
	Suitor A	1st Soldier	
	Suitor B	2nd Soldier	
	Suitor C		Driver
	Suitor D		

108

SUGGESTIONS FOR DOUBLES

| ACT III | | ACT IV | |
Scene I	Scene II	Scene I	Scene II
Reader (Act III, both scenes)		Reader (Act IV, both scenes)	
Property Man (Act III, both scenes)		Property Man (Act IV, both scenes)	
Property Man (Act III, both scenes)		Property Man (Act IV, both scenes)	
		Wang Yun	Wang Yun
		Madam Wang	Madam Wang
Warden Mu		Dragon General	Dragon General
		Tiger General	Tiger General
		Silver Stream	Silver Stream
		Golden Stream	Golden Stream
	Precious Stream	Precious Stream	Precious Stream
Gardener	Gardener		Gardener
		1st Attendant	Minister
1st and 2nd Warden		2nd Attendant	Executioner
1st West. Maid		1st Maid	1st Maid
2nd West. Maid		2nd Maid	2nd Maid
3rd West. Maid			3rd Maid
4th West. Maid			4th Maid
A.D.C. Ma Ta			A.D.C. Ma Ta
Bird & A.D.C. Kiang Hai			A.D.C. Kiang Hai
1st West. Att.			1st West. Att.
2nd West. Att.			2nd West. Att.
West. Princess			West. Princess

SCENES

ACT I

ACT II

ACT III

ACT IV

PROPERTIES

(ACTS I and II)

RIGHT STAGE. **(In prop. box or at Prop. Man's station.)**
  Prop. Box.
  5 chairs with cushions.
  Tray with wine jug and seven cups.
  Snow effect.
  50 Taels of silver.
  Embroidered ball.
  6 pillows.
  Broom.
  Dustcloth.
  Newspaper.
  Clothes brush.
  Precious Stream's dress (for change Act I).
  Firewood.
  Bag of rice.
  2 horsewhips.
  Horse effect.
  Carriage effect.
  Bundle of clothing.
  Square of blue cloth.
  Red sword.
  Teapot.
  2 teacups.
  Ashtray.
  Cigarettes.
  Matches.

OFF RIGHT
  PAVILION.
  4 lanterns.
  Carriage.

LEFT STAGE
  Prop. box.
  5 chairs with cushions.
  Teapot and 2 teacups.
  Ashtray, cigarettes and matches.

Chinese book.
Snow effect.
Inkstone, brush, and paper on tray.
6 pillows.
Newspaper.
Broom.
Dustcloth.
Chopsticks and bowl.
Small bowl.
Small stool.
Wicker basket.

OFF LEFT
  Table.

(Off stage ready for ACTS III and IV)

OFF RIGHT.
  Tray with wine pitcher and 2 cups.
  Tray with large wine pitcher and large mugs.
  Inkstand, quill pen, and paper.
  6 spears.
  The Pass.
  Cloth letter.
  Bamboo pole.
  Executioner's axe
  Handcuffs.

OFF LEFT.
  Archer's bow.
  Green sword.
  Yellow flag.
  Royal seal.
  Bamboo pole.

Prop. box.— Black wooden box, no top, 18 in. wide, 30 in long, 24 in. deep.

Chairs.—Chinese chairs.

Cushions.—Red, flat, tufted, denim, 15 in. square.

Wine jug.—Small, china, with spout.

Snow effect.—Square of black silk 30 in. rolled around stick with paper snow inside.

50 taels of silver.—Block of carved wood painted silver—to look like silver coins melted together.

Embroidered ball.—Just that, with tassel, 6 in. diameter.

Broom.—Round, rustic, with red handle.

Newspaper.—Modern Chinese daily paper.

Firewood.—Small twigs bound with cord, 15 in. long, 6 in. diameter.

Bag of rice.—White canvas, size of 5 lb. sugar bag.

Horsewhips.—1 red, 1 blue. Tassel at end, fringe every 6 in.

Horse effect.—Coco-nut shells and marble slab.

Carriage effect.—3 in. cymbals (2), on springs at end of red stick.

Bundle of clothing.—Black bag, stuffed, same size as rice bag.

Square of blue cloth.—Silk, 40 in.

Red and green swords.—Wood, in sheath, ornamentally decorated.

Bamboo pole.—5 ft. 6 in. long, painted gold.

Executioner's axe.—Wood, wide blade, silver, blue handle.

Handcuffs.—Wood, one piece, two large ovals joined together by small strip, gold colour.

Pavilion.—2 bamboo uprights, one cross piece from which hangs embroidery piece about 5 ft. 6 in. high, 6 ft. long bamboo painted gold.

Lanterns.—Wood frames, square, silk between frames, carried at end of 18 in. gold stick, electrically wired.

Small stool.—Red, 12 in. by 12 in.

Carriage.—2 squares of silk 30 in. ornate embroidered wheel in centre, attached to sticks, short handles at one end to carry with.

Inkstone.—Flat, soapstone, small depression in it for mixing ink and water, 4 in. square. Dark colour.

Table.—Black, wood, 24 in. wide, 36 in. long, 30 in. high.

The Pass.—Cloth, blue and white bricks, small doors in centre. 5 ft. 6 in. high, 5 ft. wide. Sticks at sides of pass and doors to help keep rigid.

Cloth letter.—White silk, 12 in. by 6 in., red characters on it.

Archer's bow.—Ornate gold bow, no string.

Yellow flag.—24 in. square on stick.

Royal seal.—6 in. block, covered with red cloth, drawn together and knotted at top.

MUSIC CUES

Record Part		ACT I
2		On cue from STAGE MANAGER (used to allow latecomers in audience to be seated, after READER is finished).
1	GONG NO. 4	—Wang's entrance. Stop when WANG starts to speak.
3	MADAM	—'I will come.' Stop when MADAM starts to speak.
1	GENERALS	—'Yes, we are coming.' Stop when GENERALS start to speak.
3	GENERALS	—'Thank you.' Stop when GOLDEN STREAM starts to speak.
3	SILVER S.	—'. . . she is coming.' Stop when PRECIOUS STREAM starts to speak.
3	WANG	—'Serve the feast here.' (On cue from STAGE MANAGER fade and increase volume to avoid drowning out actors.) Stop when WANG starts to speak about snow.
3	PRECIOUS S.	—'Allow me.' Stop when PRECIOUS STREAM hands HSIEH brush.
2	WANG	—'Let us retire.' (On cue from STAGE MANAGER fade and increase.) Stop when PRECIOUS STREAM starts to speak.

2	MAID	—'The will of God.' Stop at exit.
1	STAGE MGR.	—Start on cue from STAGE MANAGER. Stop as WANG starts to speak.
3	ATTENDANT	—'Come in please.' Stop as PRECIOUS STREAM starts to speak.
3	PRECIOUS S.	—'Lead the way to the pavilion.' Stop when PRECIOUS STREAM starts to speak.
3	WANG	—'Woe is the day.' Stop when all are seated.
2	WANG	—'Let us retire.' Stop when all exit.

ACT II

1	GONG NO. 3	—Entrance of SOLDIERS. Stop when SOLDIERS start to speak.
2	PRECIOUS S.	—'Oh, he has gone.' Stop as PRECIOUS STREAM exits.
3	STAGE MGR.	—Start on cue from STAGE MANAGER. Stop when MADAM speaks.
2	PRECIOUS S.	—'Oh, she has gone.' Stop as PRECIOUS STREAM exits.

ACT III

1	GONG NO. 3	—HSIEH's entrance. Stop when he speaks.
3	PRINCESS	—'To hear is to obey.' Stop when PRINCESS speaks.
3	HSIEH	—'Serve the wine in large cups.' Stop when PRINCESS falls on table.

3	PRINCESS	—'To the first pass.' Stop when WARDEN speaks.
3	WARDEN	—'Soldiers, open the pass for him.' Stop when WARDEN speaks to PRINCESS.
3	PRINCESS	—'To the second pass.' Stop when WARDEN speaks.
3	WARDEN	—'Soldiers, open the pass for him.' Stop when WARDEN speaks to PRINCESS.
3	PRINCESS	—'To the third Pass.' Stop when OLD MU speaks.
3	OLD MU	-'Open the pass for him.' (Slow music.) Stop when MA TA and KIANG HAI speak.
3	PRINCESS	—'Order the troops to be encamped here.' (Slow.) Stop on exit of all.
2	HSIEH	—'Let us retire, my Queen.' Stop as they exit.

ACT IV

1	GONG NO. 3	—WANG enters. Stop when WANG starts to speak.
3	PRECIOUS S.	—'Yes, I am coming.' Stop when PRECIOUS STREAM speaks.
1	ATTENDANTS	—'Show the Generals in, please.' Stop when GENERALS speak (up stage).
3	LADIES	—'Yes, we are coming.' Stop when MADAM speaks.
1	WANG	—'Serve the wine.' (On cues from STAGE MANAGER fade and increase.) Stop as WANG sits.

2   SILVER S.   —'I don't like this act at all.'
            Stop on her exit.

1   GONG NO. 2—Cue from STAGE MANAGER.   (READER
            exit.)
            Stop when HSIEH speaks.

3   PRECIOUS S.—'To hear is to obey.'
            Stop as she speaks.

3   PRINCESS   —'To hear is to obey.'
            Stop as she speaks.

1   ATTENDANTS—'. . . requests the presence of So and
            So.'
            Stop as he speaks.

MUSIC NOTES

In the cue sheets the record has been numbered simply
for ready reference.

In general, Part 1 is used for all entrances.

Part 2 is used for all exits.

Part 3 for the drinking and pavilion scenes, and parading
to passes.

In every instance the music starts at full volume; and
in general stops with a quick fade.

ELECTRICAL PLOT

FRONT LIGHTS

6—500 watt Leko Lights.   Gelatines Nos. 3 and 112 (together).
    1 focused L. (for READER).
    1 focused R. (for READER).
    4 flooding whole forestage.

FIRST PIPE (immediately behind inner proscenium).
    16—500 watt spots.   Gelatines Nos. 3 and 112 (together).
    All focused to cover all acting areas.

SECOND PIPE (immediately back of first pipe).
    2—500 watt spots.   Gelatine No. 14 and frost, focused on branch.
    1—X-ray.   Gelatine No. 72.

THIRD PIPE (centre stage).
    6—500 watt spots.
        2 focused on Pavilion.   Gelatines No. 3 and No. 112
            (together)
        4 focused on Cherry Branch.   Gelatine No. 29 (double).

FOURTH PIPE (cyc).
    12—250 watt cyc floods overhead.   Gelatine No. 132.
    At base of cyc:
    4 sections—3 circuit cyc foots.   Gelatines, 2 No. 14, 1 No. 132.

FOOTLIGHTS

4 sections—3 circuit foots.   Gelatines, Nos. 132, 112, and 3.
All gelatine numbers are Rosco Gelatines.   Their approximate colours are:
        No. 3—Lemon-straw.
        No. 14—Orange.
        No. 29—Medium blue.
        No. 72—Bastard amber.
        No. 112—Medium Pink.
        No. 132—Medium Light blue

LIGHT CUES

AT OPENING:
        All front lights out.
        First Pipe—low reading.
        X-rays—low reading.
        Foots—out.
        Spots on branches—full up.
        All cyc lights—full up.
        Spots on pavilion—low reading.

GONG NO. 1:
        Blue foots—full up.
        L. front spot—full up.

GONG NO. 3:
        Everything—full up.

CUE FROM STAGE MANAGER:
        First Pipe—low reading.

CUE FROM STAGE MANAGER:
        First Pipe—full up.

CUE FROM STAGE MANAGER (end of act):
        Everything as at opening (leave blue foots full up)

ACT II

GONG NO. 1:
        L. front spot—full up.

GONG NO. 2:
        Everything—full up.

CUE FROM STAGE MANAGER:
        First Pipe—low reading.

CUE FROM STAGE MANAGER:
        First Pipe—full up.

CUE FROM STAGE MANAGER (end of act):
        Everything as at opening (leave blue foots full up).

ACT III

GONG NO. 1:
     R. front spot—full up.

GONG NO. 2:
     Everything—full up.

CUE FROM STAGE MANAGER:
     First Pipe—low reading.

CUE FROM STAGE MANAGER:
     First Pipe—full up.

CUE FROM STAGE MANAGER (end of act):
     Everything as at opening (leave blue foots full up).

ACT IV

GONG NO. 1:
     L. front spot—full up.

GONG NO. 2:
     Everything—full up.

CUE FROM STAGE MANAGER:
     Everything as at opening (leave blue foots full up).

GONG NO. 1:
     L. front spot—full up.

GONG NO. 2:
     Everything—full up.

ROUTINE FOR CURTAIN CALLS:
     Curtain down—Front lights dim out.
     Curtain up—Front lights—full up.
     House lights on—foots dim out.